Presented by the
Ministry to the Armed Forces
of the
Board for Mission Services

---

with the prayer that God might richly
bless your ministry as you endeavor
to serve Him

MARTIN LUTHER

The Best from All His Works

MARTIN LUTHER

The Best from All His Works

Martin Luther
Abridged and edited by Stephen Rost

THE
CHRISTIAN
CLASSICS
COLLECTION

THOMAS NELSON PUBLISHERS
Nashville

© 1989 Thomas Nelson Publishers

All rights reserved. Written permission must be secured from the publisher to use or reproduce any part of this book, except for brief quotations in critical reviews or articles.

Published in Nashville, Tennessee, by Thomas Nelson, Inc. and distributed in Canada by Lawson Falle, Ltd., Cambridge, Ontario.

ISBN 0-8407-7176-2

Printed in the United States of America.

1 2 3 4 5 — 93 92 91 90 89

Contents

Introduction 9

1   Ninety-five Theses 15

2   Psalm 23 29

3   Isaiah 53 71

4   Sermon on the Mount: the Beatitudes 93

5   John 3:16 155

6   Romans 5 185

7   That a Christian Should Bear His Cross
    with Patience 219

8   A Meditation on Christ's Passion 225

9   A Sermon on the Three Kinds of Good Life
    for the Instruction of Consciences 237

10 Letters 251

    To Hans Luther 251

To John Luther 259

To Mrs. Margaret Luther 260

To Mrs. Katharine Luther 265

To John Luther 268

11 Table Talks 271

Luther's Evaluation of His Wife 271

Greatest Thing in Death is Fear. 272

Description of the Death
    of Magdalene Luther. 272

The Love of Parents for their Children 273

Luther's Daughter Magdalene Placed
    in Coffin. 273

The Coffin is Escorted from the Home. 274

What it Takes to Understand
    the Scriptures 275

The Study of the Bible Demands
    Humility. 276

Where the Word Is There Is Contempt 277

Man's Arrogance and Self-assurance 277

God's Punishment of the Godless 278

The Trials of a Preacher and Reformer 279

Do Not Debate with Satan When Alone 280

What is Involved in a Call
    to the Ministry. 280

Every Seventh Year Brings a Change 282

Why God Places Christians
    in the World. 282

MARTIN LUTHER

❧

Introduction

The study of church history is one of the greatest intellectual endeavors to be undertaken by man. No doubt those who hate the church or are ignorant of church history will contest the importance of this particular branch of study. Yet one need only examine history beginning with Rome to see the tremendous impact the church has had on philosophy, theology, politics, law, science, and even war. Some of the greatest minds to be found, men who gave rise to great movements, or moved nations, were connected with the church in some way.

Martin Luther is the epitome of such greatness. It is difficult to fully express the importance of this man, for church history has many competitors for such a reputation: Augustine, Anselm, Aquinas, Calvin, Schliermacher, and Barth, to name a few. While these men excelled in their own ways above their contemporaries, Martin Luther stands as possibly the most influential figure since Jesus Christ. One historian has stated that no other man in history apart from Christ has had more written about him and his thought than Martin Luther.

What has made Luther such a vital link in the chain of history? One should examine his life for the answer. Born in 1483 in Eisleben, Germany, Luther grew up in a period when the intellectual climate was at a high point. The works of great men such as Augustine, Anselm, Aquinas, Peter the Lombard, Abelard, Ockham, Aristotle, and Plato, were among the primary sources of study. Logic, philosophy, science, theology, law, classical literature and languages (Greek, Latin, Hebrew), and political theory dominated the curriculum of the universities. The intellectual environment in the universities challenged young scholars to reach far and above what the typical twentieth century student must achieve. Luther grew up in this stimulating world.

Luther attended the University of Erfurt (considered one of the most influential schools of the fifteenth century), earning the bachelor of arts degree in 1502 and the master of arts degree in 1505. In 1505 he began to study law, but his heart was really drawn to theological matters. Soon he gave up the study of law and joined an Augustinian monastery in Erfurt. There he became fully immersed in the traditional Catholic faith. His great intellectual bent enabled him to master Greek and Hebrew and to commit to memory most of the New Testament. Ordained as a priest in 1507, he began his career as a university professor at Wittenberg and Erfurt, and he acquired his doctorate in 1512.

Luther became distressed at the selling of indulgences by the pope, so in 1517 he nailed his "95 Theses" to the door of the Wittenberg church. This non-combative act was the acceptable means for seeking a public discussion on the issues in dispute. The conflicts that resulted eventually led Luther to see the Bible, not the pope, as the sole authority over man. Later he became a true Christian, and from there his relationship with the Catholic church became so strained that he was excommunicated. This separation led to greater conflict, and Luther became the recognized leader of what became the Reformation. Luther's outspokenness signaled the beginning of a new movement—Protestantism—and a new period in history—the Reformation.

Luther wrote extensively on such matters as politics and theological issues in his commentaries on the Bible, sermons, devotional material, and hymns. He also translated the Bible into German. Luther died in 1546, but he left a tremendous mark on history.

His influence truly reaches beyond the sixteenth century. His clear teaching on the authority of the Bible and salvation by faith alone have relevance for Christians today and always.

What started out as a peaceful challenge to the selling of indulgences initiated one of the greatest religious movements in history. Luther's "Ninety-five Theses" (posted October 31, 1517 in Wittenberg) indirectly gave rise to Protestantism. The dominance of the Catholic church was for the first time challenged with such force that she couldn't stop it.

In the "Ninety-five Theses" Luther challenged the selling of indulgences by the Catholic church. Luther merely sought a peaceful means to communicate with Catholic authorities, but a great schism resulted, leading to Luther's excommunication and the beginning of the Reformation.

In the Theses Luther points out that, according to canon law, the pope cannot remit penalties upon souls in purgatory. Luther attacked the greed and avarice found in the Church, as well as the false teaching that men could buy their way into heaven. Luther ended the Theses by stating that Christ was the only source of salvation from hell, and that all men should cast their hope upon Him. It is no wonder that these and other charges were not taken well by the Catholic authorities.

CHAPTER ONE

Ninety-five Theses

Out of love and zeal for truth and the desire to bring it to light, the following theses will be publicly discussed at Wittenberg under the chairmanship of the Reverend Father Martin Luther, Master of Arts and Sacred Theology and regularly appointed Lecturer on these subjects at that place. He requests that those who cannot be present to debate orally with us will do so by letter.[1]

In the Name of Our Lord Jesus Christ. Amen.

1. When our Lord and Master Jesus Christ said, "Repent" (Matt. 4:17), he willed the entire life of believers to be one of repentance.

2. This word cannot be understood as referring to the

---

[1]There was actually no debate, for no one responded to the invitation. The contents of the ninety-five theses were soon widely disseminated by word of mouth and by the printers, and in effect a vigorous debate took place that lasted for a number of years.

sacrament of penance, that is, confession and satisfaction, as administered by the clergy.

3. Yet it does not mean solely inner repentance; such inner repentance is worthless unless it produces various outward mortifications of the flesh.

4. The penalty of sin[2] remains as long as the hatred of self, that is, true inner repentance, until our entrance into the kingdom of heaven.

5. The pope neither desires nor is able to remit any penalties except those imposed by his own authority or that of the canons.[3]

6. The pope cannot remit any guilt, except by declaring and showing that it has been remitted by God; or, to be sure, by remitting guilt in cases reserved to his [the pope's] judgment. If his right to grant remission in these cases were disregarded, the guilt would certainly remain unforgiven.

7. God remits guilt to no one unless at the same time he humbles him in all things and makes him submissive to his vicar, the priest.

8. The penitential canons are imposed only on the living, and, according to the canons themselves, nothing should be imposed on the dying.

9. Therefore, the Holy Spirit through the pope is kind to us insofar as the pope in his decrees always makes exception of the article of death and of necessity.[4]

10. Those priests act ignorantly and wickedly who, in

---

[2]Catholic theology distinguishes between the "guilt" and the "penalty" of sin.

[3]The canons, or decrees of the church, have the force of law. Those referred to here and in Theses 8 and 85 are the so-called penitential canons.

[4]Commenting on this thesis in the *Explanations of the Ninety-five Theses,* Luther distinguishes between temporal and eternal necessity. "Necessity knows no law." "Death is the necessity of necessities."

the case of the dying, reserve canonical penalties for purgatory.

11. Those tares of changing the canonical penalty to the penalty of purgatory were evidently sown while the bishops slept (Matt. 13:25).

12. In former times canonical penalties were imposed, not after, but before absolution, as tests of true contrition.

13. The dying are freed by death from all penalties, are already dead as far as the canon laws are concerned, and have a right to be released from them.

14. Imperfect piety or love on the part of the dying person necessarily brings with it great fear; and the smaller the love, the greater the fear.

15. This fear or horror is sufficient in itself, to say nothing of other things, to constitute the penalty of purgatory, since it is very near the horror of despair.

16. Hell, purgatory, and heaven seem to differ the same as despair, fear, and assurance of salvation.

17. It seems as though for the souls in purgatory fear should necessarily decrease and love increase.

18. Furthermore, it does not seem proved, either by reason or Scripture, that souls in purgatory are outside the state of merit, that is, unable to grow in love.

19. Nor does it seem proved that souls in purgatory, at least not all of them, are certain and assured of their own salvation, even if we ourselves may be entirely certain of it.

20. Therefore, the pope, when he uses the words "plenary remission of all penalties," does not actually mean "all penalties," but only those imposed by himself.

21. Thus those indulgence preachers are in error who

say that a man is absolved from every penalty and saved by papal indulgences.

22. As a matter of fact, the pope remits to souls in purgatory no penalty which, according to canon law, they should have paid in this life.

23. If remission of all penalties whatsoever could be granted to anyone at all, certainly it would be granted only to the most perfect, that is, to very few.

24. For this reason most people are necessarily deceived by that indiscriminate and high-sounding promise of release from penalty.

25. That power which the pope has in general over purgatory corresponds to the power which any bishop or curate has in a particular way in his own diocese or parish.

26. The pope does very well when he grants remission to souls in purgatory, not by the power of the keys, which he does not have,[5] but by way of intercession for them.

27. They preach only human doctrines who say that as soon as the money clinks into the money chest, the soul flies out of purgatory.

28. It is certain that when money clinks in the money chest, greed and avarice can be increased; but when the church intercedes, the result is in the hands of God alone.

29. Who knows whether all souls in purgatory wish to be redeemed, since we have exceptions in Saint Severinus and Saint Paschal,[6] as related in a legend.

---

[5]This is not a denial of the power of the keys, that is, the power to forgive and to retain sin, but merely an assertion that the power of the keys does not extend to purgatory.

[6]The legend is to the effect that these saints, Pope Severinus (638–640) and Pope Paschal I (817–824), preferred to remain longer in purgatory that they might have greater glory in heaven.

30. No one is sure of the integrity of his own contrition, much less of having received plenary remission.

31. The man who actually buys indulgences is as rare as he who is really penitent; indeed, he is exceedingly rare.

32. Those who believe that they can be certain of their salvation because they have indulgence letters will be eternally damned, together with their teachers.

33. Men must especially be on their guard against those who say that the pope's pardons are that inestimable gift of God by which man is reconciled to him.

34. For the graces of indulgences are concerned only with the penalties of sacramental satisfaction[7] established by man.

35. They who teach that contrition is not necessary on the part of those who intend to buy souls out of purgatory or to buy confessional privileges[8] preach unchristian doctrine.

36. Any truly repentant Christian has a right to full remission of penalty and guilt,[9] even without indulgence letters.

37. Any true Christian, whether living or dead, participates in all the blessings of Christ and the church; and

---

[7]Satisfaction is that act on the part of the penitent, in connection with the sacrament of penance, by means of which he pays the temporal penalty for his sins. If at death he is in arrears in paying his temporal penalty for venial sins, he pays this penalty in purgatory. Indulgences are concerned with this satisfaction of the sacrament of penance—they permit a partial or complete (plenary) remission of temporal punishment. According to Roman Catholic theology, the buyer of an indulgence still has to confess his sins, be absolved from them, and be truly penitent.

[8]These are privileges entitling the holder of indulgence letters to choose his own confessor and relieving him, the holder, of certain satisfactions.

[9]To justify the placing of absolution before satisfaction, contrary to the practice of the early church, theologians distinguished between the guilt and the penalty of sins.

this is granted him by God, even without indulgence letters.

38. Nevertheless, papal remission and blessing are by no means to be disregarded, for they are, as I have said [Thesis 6], the proclamation of the divine remission.

39. It is very difficult, even for the most learned theologians, at one and the same time to commend to the people the bounty of indulgences and the need of true contrition.

40. A Christian who is truly contrite seeks and loves to pay penalties for his sins; the bounty of indulgences, however, relaxes penalties and causes men to hate them—at least it furnishes occasion for hating them.

41. Papal indulgences must be preached with caution, lest people erroneously think that they are preferable to other good works of love.

42. Christians are to be taught that the pope does not intend that the buying of indulgences should in any way be compared with works of mercy.

43. Christians are to be taught that he who gives to the poor or lends to the needy does a better deed than he who buys indulgences.

44. Because love grows by works of love, man thereby becomes better. Man does not, however, become better by means of indulgences but is merely freed from penalties.

45. Christians are to be taught that he who sees a needy man and passes him by, yet gives his money for indulgences, does not buy papal indulgences but God's wrath.

46. Christians are to be taught that, unless they have more than they need, they must reserve enough for their

family needs and by no means squander it on indulgences.

47. Christians are to be taught that the buying of indulgences is a matter of free choice, not commanded.

48. Christians are to be taught that the pope, in granting indulgences, needs and thus desires their devout prayer more than their money.

49. Christians are to be taught that papal indulgences are useful only if they do not put their trust in them, but very harmful if they lose their fear of God because of them.

50. Christians are to be taught that if the pope knew the exactions of the indulgence preachers, he would rather that the basilica of Saint Peter were burned to ashes than built up with the skin, flesh, and bones of his sheep.

51. Christians are to be taught that the pope would and should wish to give of his own money, even though he had to sell the basilica of Saint Peter, to many of those from whom certain hawkers of indulgences cajole money.

52. It is vain to trust in salvation by indulgence letters, even though the indulgence commissary, or even the pope, were to offer his soul as security.

53. They are enemies of Christ and the pope who forbid altogether the preaching of the Word of God in some churches in order that indulgences may be preached in others.

54. Injury is done the Word of God when, in the same sermon, an equal or larger amount of time is devoted to indulgences than to the Word.

55. It is certainly the pope's sentiment that if indulgences, which are a very insignificant thing, are cele-

brated with one bell, one procession, and one ceremony, then the gospel, which is the very greatest thing, should be preached with a hundred bells, a hundred processions, a hundred ceremonies.

56. The treasures of the church,[10] out of which the pope distributes indulgences, are not sufficiently discussed or known among the people of Christ.

57. That indulgences are not temporal treasures is certainly clear, for many indulgence sellers do not distribute them freely but only gather them.

58. Nor are they the merits of Christ and the saints, for, even without the pope, the latter always work grace for the inner man, and the cross, death, and hell for the outer man.

59. Saint Laurence said that the poor of the church were the treasures of the church, but he spoke according to the usage of the word in his own time.

60. Without want of consideration we say that the keys of the church,[11] given by the merits of Christ, are that treasure;

61. For it is clear that the pope's power is of itself sufficient for the remission of penalties and cases reserved by himself.

62. The true treasure of the church is the most holy gospel of the glory and grace of God.

63. But this treasure is naturally most odious, for it makes the first to be last (Matt. 20:16).

64. On the other hand, the treasure of indulgences is

---

[10]The treasury of merits is a reserve fund of good works accumulated by Christ and the saints upon which the pope could draw when he remitted satisfaction in indulgences.

[11]The office of the keys: the preaching of the gospel, the celebrating of the sacraments, the remitting of sins to the penitent, and the excommunicating of impenitent sinners.

naturally most acceptable, for it makes the last to be first.

65. Therefore, the treasures of the gospel are nets with which one formerly fished for men of wealth.

66. The treasures of indulgences are nets with which one now fishes for the wealth of men.

67. The indulgences which the demagogues acclaim as the greatest graces are actually understood to be such only insofar as they promote gain.

68. They are nevertheless in truth the most insignificant graces when compared with the grace of God and the piety of the cross.

69. Bishops and curates are bound to admit the commissaries of papal indulgences with all reverence.

70. But they are much more bound to strain their eyes and ears lest these men preach their own dreams instead of what the pope has commissioned.

71. Let him who speaks against the truth concerning papal indulgences be anathema and accursed;

72. But let him who guards against the lust and license of the indulgence preachers be blessed;

73. Just as the pope justly thunders against those who by any means whatsoever contrive harm to the sale of indulgences.

74. But much more does he intend to thunder against those who use indulgences as a pretext to contrive harm to holy love and truth.

75. To consider papal indulgences so great that they could absolve a man even if he had done the impossible and had violated the mother of God is madness.

76. We say on the contrary that papal indulgences cannot remove the very least of venial sins as far as guilt is concerned.

77. To say that even Saint Peter, if he were now pope,

could not grant greater graces is blasphemy against Saint Peter and the pope.

78. We say on the contrary that even the present pope, or any pope whatsoever, has greater graces at his disposal, that is, the gospel, spiritual powers, gifts of healing, etc., as it is written in 1 Corinthians 12:28.

79. To say that the cross emblazoned with the papal coat of arms, and set up by the indulgence preachers, is equal in worth to the cross of Christ is blasphemy.

80. The bishops, curates, and theologians who permit such talk to be spread among the people will have to answer for this.

81. This unbridled preaching of indulgences makes it difficult even for learned men to rescue the reverence which is due the pope from slander or from the shrewd questions of the laity,

82. Such as, "Why does not the pope empty purgatory for the sake of holy love and the dire need of the souls that are there if he redeems an infinite number of souls for the sake of miserable money with which to build a church? The former reasons would be most just; the latter is most trivial."

83. Again, "Why are funeral and anniversary masses for the dead continued and why does he not return or permit the withdrawal of the endowments founded for them, since it is wrong to pray for the redeemed?"

84. Again, "What is this new piety of God and the pope that for a consideration of money they permit a man who is impious and their enemy to buy out of purgatory the pious soul of a friend of God and do not rather, because of the need of that pious and beloved soul, free it for pure love's sake?"

85. Again, "Why are the penitential canons, long since

abrogated and dead in actual fact and through disuse, now satisfied by the granting of indulgences as though they were still alive and in force?"

86. Again, "Why does not the pope, whose wealth is today greater than the wealth of the richest Crassus,[12] build this one basilica of Saint Peter with his own money rather than with the money of poor believers?"

87. Again, "What does the pope remit or grant to those who by perfect contrition already have a right to full remission and blessings?"[13]

88. Again, "What greater blessing could come to the church than if the pope were to bestow these remissions and blessings on every believer a hundred times a day, as he now does but once?"[14]

89. "Since the pope seeks the salvation of souls rather than money by his indulgences, why does he suspend the indulgences and pardons previously granted when they have equal efficacy?"[15]

90. To repress these very sharp arguments of the laity by force alone, and not to resolve them by giving reasons, is to expose the church and the pope to the ridicule of their enemies and to make Christians unhappy.

91. If, therefore, indulgences were preached according to the spirit and intention of the pope, all these doubts would be readily resolved. Indeed, they would not exist.

---

[12]Marcus Licinius Crassus (115–53 B.C.), also called Dives ("the Rich"), was noted for his wealth and luxury by the classical Romans. Crassus means "the Fat."

[13]See Theses 36 and 37.

[14]The indulgence letter entitled its possessor to receive absolution once during his lifetime and once at the approach of death.

[15]During the time when the jubilee indulgences were preached, other indulgences were suspended.

92. Away then with all those prophets who say to the people of Christ, "Peace, peace," and there is no peace! (Jer. 6:14).

93. Blessed be all those prophets who say to the people of Christ, "Cross, cross," and there is no cross!

94. Christians should be exhorted to be diligent in following Christ, their head, through penalties, death, and hell;

95. And thus be confident of entering into heaven through many tribulations rather than through the false security of peace (Acts 14:22).

With the possible exception of John 3:16, no other passage in the Bible is better known than Psalm 23. This popular passage has brought hope even to the unregenerate.

Luther cited this passage as a source of comfort to Christians in the midst of struggles. Because Christ is the Shepherd who cares for His flock, He seeks to provide what is best for His sheep. A child of God can rely on the fresh provisions the Shepherd supplies. Protection from would-be destroyers provides peace for the soul. Even the discipline of the rod is indicative of the Shepherd's great love and care. Without these benefits, the sheep would be hopelessly lost.

CHAPTER TWO

Psalm 23

The Lord is my Shepherd, I shall not want.

First of all the prophet, and every believing heart, calls God his Shepherd. Scripture gives God many friendly names, but especially dear and charming is the one that the prophet gives God here in calling Him a Shepherd and saying, "The Lord is my Shepherd." It is most comforting when Scripture calls God our refuge, our strength, our rock, our fortress, shield, hope, our comfort, Savior, King. For by His actions and without ceasing, He truly demonstrates in His people that He is exactly as Scripture portrays Him. It is exceedingly comforting to know, however, that here and in other places in Scripture He is frequently called a Shepherd. For in this single little word "shepherd" there are gathered together in one almost all the good and comforting things that we praise in God.

The prophet therefore uses these words with a happy, secure heart—a heart that is filled with faith and overflows with great joy and comfort. He does not say, "The Lord is my strength, fortress," which would also be very comforting, but "my Shepherd"; as though he would say, "If the Lord is my Shepherd and I am His sheep, then I am very well supplied both in body and soul. He will feed me well, protect and preserve me from misfortune, care for me, help me out of all troubles, comfort me, and strengthen me. In short, He will do for me what a good shepherd can be expected to do." All of these blessings, and more, are comprehended in the single little word "shepherd"; and so he himself soon interprets it when he says, "I shall not want." Some of the other names which Scripture gives God sound almost too splendid and majestic and at once arouse awe and fear when we hear them mentioned; for example, when Scripture calls God our Lord, King, Creator. The little word "shepherd," however, is not of that kind but has a very friendly sound. When the devout read or hear it, it immediately grants them a confidence, a comfort, and a sense of security that the word "father" and others grant when they are attributed to God.

Therefore this metaphor is one of the most beautiful and comforting and yet most common of all in Scripture, when it compares His Divine Majesty to a pious, faithful, or as Christ says, "good shepherd" (John 10:14), and compares us poor, weak, miserable sinners to sheep. One can, however, understand this comforting and beautiful picture best when one goes to nature, from which the prophets have taken this picture and similar ones, and carefully learns from it the traits and characteristics of a natural sheep and the office, the work, and the care of a pious shepherd. Whoever does this carefully will not only readily understand this comparison and others in Scripture concerning the shepherd and the sheep, but will also find the comparisons exceedingly sweet and comforting.

A sheep must live entirely by its shepherd's help, protection, and care. As soon as it loses him, it is surrounded by all kinds of dangers and must perish, for it is quite unable to help itself. The reason? It is a poor, weak, simple little beast that can neither feed nor rule itself, nor find the right way, nor protect itself against any kind of danger or misfortune. Moreover, it is by nature timid, shy, and likely to go astray. When it does go a bit astray and leaves its shepherd, it is unable to find its way back to him; indeed, it merely runs farther away from him. Though it may find other shepherds and sheep, that does not help it, for it does not know the voices of strange shepherds. Therefore it flees them and strays about until the wolf seizes it or it perishes some other way.

Still, however weak and small an animal a sheep may be, it nevertheless has this trait about it: it is very careful to stay near its shepherd, take comfort in his help and protection, and follow him however and wherever he may lead it. And if it can only so much as be near him, it worries about nothing, fears no one, and is secure and happy; for it lacks absolutely nothing. It also has this virtue—and this is to be marked well, because Christ praises it especially in His sheep (John 10:4)—that it very carefully and surely hears and knows its shepherd's voice, is guided by it, does not let itself be turned away from it, but follows it without swerving. On the other hand, it pays no attention at all to the voices of strange shepherds. Though they may tempt and lure it in the most friendly manner, it does not heed them, much less does it follow them.

It is the function of a faithful shepherd not only to supply his sheep with good pasture and other related things, but also to keep them from suffering harm. Moreover, he takes good care not to lose any of them. But if one of them should go astray, he goes after it, seeks it, and returns it (Luke 15:4). He looks after the young, the weak, and the sick very carefully, waits on them, lifts them up and carries them in his arms (Isa. 40:11) until they are grown and are strong and well.

Just so it is in spiritual shepherding, that is, in Christendom. As little as a natural sheep can feed, direct, guide itself, or guard and protect itself against danger and misfortune—for it is a weak and quite defenseless little animal—just so little can we poor, weak, miserable people feed and guide ourselves spiritually, walk and remain on the right path, or by our own power protect ourselves against all evil and gain help and comfort for ourselves in anxiety and distress.

How shall a man be able to govern himself in a God-pleasing manner when he knows nothing of God, is born and conceived in sin (Ps. 51:5), as we all are, and is by nature a child of wrath (Eph. 2:3) and an enemy of God? How shall we find the right path and stay on it when, as Isaiah says (Isa. 63:6), we cannot do otherwise than go astray? How is it possible for us to defend ourselves against the devil, who is a prince and ruler of this world and whose captives we all are, when with all our strength and power we cannot keep even a little leaf from hurting us or even command a weak fly? Why should we poor, miserable people desire to boast loudly of great comfort, help, and counsel against the judgments of God, the wrath of God, and eternal death, when every day and every hour we experience in ourselves and in others that even in trivial, bodily needs we can neither counsel and help ourselves nor seek comfort?

Let us therefore conclude freely [that] as little as a natural sheep can help itself in even the slightest degree but must simply depend on its shepherd for all benefits, just so little—and much less—can a man govern himself and find comfort, help, and counsel in himself in the things that pertain to his salvation. He must depend on God, his Shepherd, for all of that. And God is a thousand times more willing to do everything that is to be done for His sheep than is any faithful human shepherd.

This Shepherd, however, of whom the prophet foretold so long before, is Christ, our dear Lord, who is a Shepherd much different from Moses. Moses is harsh and unfriendly toward his sheep. He drives them away into the desert, where they will find neither pasture nor water but only want (Exod. 3:1). Christ, however, is the good, friendly Shepherd, who goes after a famished and lost sheep in the wilderness, seeks it there, and, when He has found it, lays it on His shoulder rejoicing (Luke 15:4). He even "gives His life for His sheep" (John 10:12). He is a friendly Shepherd. Who would not be happy to be His sheep?

The voice of this Shepherd, however, with which He speaks to His sheep and calls them, is the holy Gospel. It teaches us how we may win grace, forgiveness of sins, and eternal salvation: not by the law of Moses, which makes us even more shy, unstable, and discouraged, though even in times past we were excessively timid, shy, and frightened; but by Christ, who is "the Shepherd and Bishop of our souls" (1 Pet. 2:25). For Christ has sought us miserable, lost sheep and has brought us back from the wilderness. That is, He has redeemed us from the law, sin, death, the power of the devil, and eternal damnation. By giving His life for us He has obtained for us grace, forgiveness of sin, comfort, help, strength, and eternal life against the devil and all misfortune. To the sheep of Christ this is a dear, sweet voice. They are sincerely glad to hear it, for they know it well and let themselves be guided by it. But a strange voice they neither know nor hear, because it sounds unfamiliar; they avoid it and flee for it (John 10:5).

The pasture with which Christ feeds His sheep is also the dear gospel, by which our souls are fed and strengthened, preserved from error, comforted in all temptations and sorrows, protected against the devil's wile and power, and finally saved from all need. But His sheep are not all equally strong; in part they are still lost, scattered hither and yon, wounded, sick, young, and weak. He does not reject them for that reason but actually gives more attention to them and also cares for them more diligently than He does for the others who have no faults. As the prophet Ezekiel says in his thirty-fourth chapter (Ezek. 34:16), He seeks the lost, brings back the strayed, binds up the crippled, strengthens the sick. And the young lambs that have just been born, says Isaiah (40:11), He will gather in His arms and carry them so that they may not grow tired, and will gently lead those that are with young. All of this, Christ, our dear Shepherd, effects through the office of preaching and the holy sacraments, as is taught elsewhere frequently and with many words. It would take too long and require too many words to emphasize all these things adequately at this place. Besides, the prophet will indicate them later in the psalm.

From these words we can also see clearly how shamefully we have been led astray under the papacy. It did not depict Christ in so friendly a fashion as did the dear prophets, apostles, and Christ Himself, but portrayed Him so horribly that we were more afraid of Him than of Moses and thought that the teaching of Moses was much easier and more friendly than the teaching of Christ. Therefore, we knew Christ only as an angry judge, whose anger we had to reconcile with our good works and holy life and whose grace we had to obtain through the merit and intercession of the dear saints. That is a shameful lie that not only deceives poor consciences miserably but also profanes God's grace to the extreme, denies Christ's death, resurrection, ascension into heaven, together with all His inexpressible blessings, blasphemes and damns His holy gospel, destroys faith, and sets up in its place nothing but horror, lies, and error.

If that is not darkness, then I do not know what darkness is. Up to now no one was able to notice it, but everyone considered it the pure truth. To the present day our papists wish to have it preserved as right and hence shed much innocent blood. Dear friend, if we can feed and rule ourselves, protect ourselves against error, gain grace and forgiveness of sins through our own merit, resist the devil and all misfortune, conquer sin and death—then all Scripture must be a lie when it testifies of us that we are lost, scattered, wounded, weak, and defenseless sheep. Then we do not need a Christ either as a Shepherd who would seek, gather, and direct us, bind up our wounds, watch over us, and strengthen us against the devil. Then He has also given His life for us in vain. For as long as we can do and gain all these things through our own powers and piety, we do not need the help of Christ at all.

But here at once you hear the opposite, namely, that you lost sheep cannot find your way to the Shepherd yourself but can only roam around in the wilderness. If

Christ, your Shepherd, did not seek you and bring you back, you would simply have to fall prey to the wolf. But now He comes, seeks, and finds you. He takes you into His flock, that is, into Christendom, through the Word and the sacrament. He gives His life for you, keeps you always on the right path, so that you may not fall into error. You hear nothing at all about your powers, good works, and merits—unless you would say that it is strength, good works, merit when you run around in the wilderness and are defenseless and lost. No, Christ alone is active here, merits things, and manifests His power. He seeks, carries, and directs you. He earns life for you through His death. He alone is strong and keeps you from perishing, from being snatched out of His hand (John 10:28). And for all of this you can do nothing at all but only lend your ears, hear, and with thanksgiving receive the inexpressible treasure, and learn to know well the voice of your Shepherd, follow Him, and avoid the voice of the stranger.

If you wish, therefore, to be richly supplied in both body and soul, then, above all, give careful attention to the voice of this Shepherd; listen to His words, let Him feed, direct, lead, protect, and comfort you. That is, hold fast to His Word, hear and learn it gladly, for then you will be well supplied in both body and soul.

From what has been said until now, I hope one can easily understand these words, "The Lord is my Shepherd," and indeed the whole psalm. The words "The Lord is my Shepherd" are brief but also very impressive and apt. The world glories and trusts in honor, power, riches, and the favor of men. Our psalm, however, glories in none of these, for they are all uncertain and perishable. It says briefly, "The Lord is my Shepherd." Thus speaks a sure, certain faith that turns its back on everything temporal and transitory, however noble and precious it may be, and turns its face and heart directly to the Lord, who alone is Lord and is and does everything. "He and none other, be he a king or an emperor, is my Shepherd," the psalmist says. Therefore he speaks out freely and with all boldness and says,

I shall not want.

Thus the prophet speaks, in a general way, of the various kinds of bodily and spiritual blessings that we receive through the office of preaching. It is as though he would say, "If the Lord is my Shepherd, then of course I shall not want. I shall have an abundance of meat, drink, clothing, food, protection, peace, and of all the necessities that pertain to the preservation of this life. For I have a rich Shepherd who will not let me suffer want." Chiefly, however, he speaks of the spiritual possessions and gifts that God's Word provides and says, "Because the Lord has taken me into His flock and provides me with His pasture and care, that is, because He has richly given me His holy Word, He will not let me want anywhere. He will bless His Word so that it may be effective and bring forth fruit in me. He will also give me His Spirit, who will assist and comfort me in all temptations and distresses and will also make my heart safe and sure. My heart, therefore, will not doubt that I am my Lord's dear sheep and that He is my faithful Shepherd. He will treat me gently as His poor, weak sheep. He will strengthen my faith and provide me with other spiritual gifts; comfort me in all my troubles; hear me when I call upon Him; keep the wolf, that is, the devil, from being able to do me harm; and finally redeem me from all misfortune." This is what the psalmist has in mind when he says, "I shall not want."

"Yes," you may say, "but how shall I know that the Lord is my Shepherd? I have not experienced that He is as friendly toward me as the psalm says; in fact, I have experienced the opposite. David was a holy prophet and a man dear and precious to God, so it was easy for him to speak of the matter and to believe what he spoke. But I cannot emulate him, for I am a poor sinner." Answer: I have shown above that in itself a sheep has chiefly this good attribute and fine virtue, that it knows the voice of its shepherd well and is guided more by its ears than its eyes. The same virtue Christ also praises in His sheep, when He says, "My sheep know My voice" (John 10:4), His voice, however, speaks thus, "I am the Good Shepherd . . . and lay down My life for My sheep. . . . And I give them eternal life. And they shall never perish, and no man shall snatch them out of My hand" (John 10:14, 15, 28). Give careful attention to this voice and be guided by it. If you do, then firmly believe that you are Christ's sheep and that He is your Shepherd, who knows you well and is also able to call you by your name. But when you have Him as your Shepherd, you will surely not want. Yes, you already have what you shall have—eternal life. Nor will you ever perish. Nor shall any power be so great and mighty that it could snatch you out of His hand. Of that you can be sure. For this Shepherd's voice will surely not lead you astray. What more could you want?

But if you ignore this voice and are guided by what your eyes see and your old Adam feels, then you will lose the faith and the confidence that you ought, as a sheep, to have in Him as your Shepherd. Sometimes this thought, sometimes that one comes to you, so that you cannot be content but must argue with yourself and say, "If the Lord is my Shepherd, why does He impose this upon me, that the world torments and persecutes me so cruelly through no fault of mine? I am sitting in the midst of the wolves, I am not sure of my life for a moment; but I do not see any shepherd who would protect me." Again, "Why does He permit the devil to harm me so greatly with terror and doubts? Besides, I find myself quite unfit, weak, impatient, still laden with many sins. I feel no security but only doubt, no comfort but only fear and trembling because of God's wrath. When will He ever begin to manifest in me that He is my Shepherd?"

Such strange thoughts and many others will come to you if you fail to heed His voice and Word. But if you hold fast to them, you will be tempted neither by the devil's wile, the world's disfavor and raging, nor by your own weakness and unworthiness. You will go straight forward to speak freely, "Let the devil, the world, or my own conscience oppose me as violently as they may. I will not for that reason grieve myself to death. It must be so and it shall be so, that whoever is the Lord's sheep will surely be assailed by the wolves. Be it with me as it may, let them boil or roast me, it shall be my comfort that my Shepherd has given His life for me. Moreover, He has a sweet, kind voice with which He comforts me and says that I shall never perish, neither shall any man snatch me out of His hand; I shall have eternal life (John 10:28). And He will keep this promise, no matter what happens to me. If because of my weakness some sin or other fault by chance is still found in me, he will not reject me on that account. For He is a friendly Shepherd, who watches over the weak sheep, binds up their wounds, and heals them. And so that I may be all the more sure and not doubt, He has given me, as a token, His holy sacraments."

Just so it was with the prophet. He was not always

happy, nor was he at all times able to sing, "The Lord is my Shepherd, I shall not want." At times he wanted much, almost too much. He would feel neither justice nor God's comfort and help, but only sin, God's wrath, terror, doubt, and the fear of hell, as he laments in many psalms. Nevertheless he abandons his feelings and holds God to His promise of a coming Messiah and thinks, "Be it with me as it may. This is still the comfort of my heart, that I have a gracious, merciful Lord, who is my Shepherd, whose Word and promise strengthen and comfort me. Therefore I shall not want." For this reason also he wrote this psalm and others, that we might be sure that in real temptation we can find counsel and comfort nowhere else, and that this alone is the golden art: to cling to God's Word and promise, to make judgments on the basis of this Word and not on the basis of the feelings of the heart. Then help and comfort will surely follow, and absolutely nothing will be wanting. The second verse follows.

He feeds me in a green pasture and leads me to the fresh water.

In the first verse the prophet briefly gathered together the meaning of the whole psalm, namely, that whoever has the Lord as a Shepherd will not want. He does not teach anything more in this psalm, but he does emphasize the thought further by means of fine figurative words and pictures and shows how it comes about that those who are the Lord's sheep want nothing, and says, "He feeds me." Through almost the entire psalm, as he often does elsewhere, he uses words with a meaning different from their literal one. When he mentions the shepherd, the pasture, the green meadow, the fresh water, the rod, and the staff, therefore, we may well conclude that he wants something else to be understood by these words than we human beings are in the habit of saying with them. Such a way of speaking is very common in Scripture, and therefore we should make every effort to get accustomed to it and learn to understand it.

But see how beautifully he can speak! "I am," he says, "the Lord's sheep; He feeds me in a green pasture." For a natural sheep nothing can be better than when its shepherd feeds it in pleasant green pastures and near fresh water. Where that happens to it, it feels that no one on earth is richer and more blessed than it is. For it finds there whatever it might desire: fine, lush, heavy grass, from which it will grow strong and fat; fresh water, with which it can refresh and restore itself whenever it likes; and it has its joy and pleasure there too. At this point David would also say that God had shown him no greater grace and blessing on earth than this, that he was permitted to be at a place and among people where God's Word and dwelling place and the right worship were to be found. There these treasures are found, there things prosper well, both in the spiritual and in the secular realm. It is as if he were saying, "All people and kingdoms on earth are nothing. They may be richer, more powerful, and more splendid than we Jews, and they may also boast mightily of what they have. Moreover, they may glory in their wisdom and holiness, for they, too, have gods whom they serve. But with all their glory and splendor they are a mere desert and wilderness. For they have neither shepherd nor pasture, and therefore, the sheep must go astray, famish, and perish. But though we are surrounded by many deserts, we can sit and rest here, safe and happy in paradise and in a pleasant green pasture, where there is an abundance of grass and of fresh water and where we have our Shepherd near us, who feeds us, leads us to the watering place, and protects us. Therefore, we cannot want."

That man had spiritual eyes and therefore saw plainly what is the best and noblest thing on earth. He does not glory in his royal splendor and power, for he knows well that such possessions are gifts of God. He does not run away from them either and let them lie idle, but uses them to the glory of God and thanks God for them. Above all he glories in this, that the Lord is his Shepherd and that he is in His pasture and in His care, that is, that he has God's Word. This blessing he can never forget, but speaks about it very beautifully and with great joy, and praises it far above all possessions on earth, as he also does in many other psalms. Thus he says, "The word of Thy mouth is dearer to me than thousands of gold and silver pieces" (Ps. 119:72), and, also, "It is more precious than gold, even much fine gold; sweeter also than honey and drippings of the honeycomb" (Ps. 19:11).

We too should learn this art, namely, to let the world glory forever in great riches, honor, and power. For these are indeed loose, uncertain, perishable wares that God lets men scramble for. It is a simple thing for Him to give to a scoundrel—who in turn blasphemes and slanders Him—a kingdom, a principality, or other honors and possessions on this earth. These are His chaff and His husks, with which He fills the bellies of His sows that He is about to slaughter (Luke 15:16). To His children, however, as David says here, He gives the genuine treasure. Therefore, as the dear children and heirs of God, we ought to glory in neither our wisdom, nor strength, nor riches, but in this, that we have the "pearl of great value" (Matt. 13:46), the dear Word, through which we know God, our dear Father, and Jesus Christ, whom He has sent (John 17:3). That is our treasure and heritage, and it is sure and eternal and better than all worldly possessions. Whoever has this treasure may let others gather money, live riotously, be proud and haughty. Let him not be troubled by such things, though he be despised and poor in the eyes of the world. But let him thank God for His inexpressible gift (2 Cor. 9:15) and pray that he may abide by it.

It does not matter how rich and glorious we are here on earth; if we keep this treasure, we are exceedingly rich and sufficiently honored. Saint Paul was an unworthy, miserable man on earth, and the devil and the world assailed him most violently. To God he was a dear, worthy man. He was so poor, too, that he had to provide for himself with the work of his hands. And yet, despite such great poverty, he was richer than the emperor in Rome, though he had no other riches than the knowledge of Christ, in comparison with which, he says, "I count all things (nothing on earth is excluded) but loss and refuse" (Phil. 3:8).

May our dear God grant us grace that we, too, like David, Paul, and other saints, regard our treasure, which is the very same one they had, as something great and exalt it above all possessions on earth and thank God sincerely for having honored us with it above many other thousands. He might just as well have let us go astray as the Turks, Tartars, Jews, and other infidels, who know nothing of the treasure. He might have let us remain hardened like the papists, who blaspheme and damn our treasure. It is only because of His grace, however, that He has placed us into His green pastures and has provided us so richly with good food and fresh water. Therefore we should thank Him all the more.

The prophet, however, calls God's people and the holy

Christian church a "green pasture," for it is God's pleasure ground, decorated and adorned with all kinds of
spiritual gifts. The pasture, however, or the grass in it, is
God's Word, with which our consciences are strengthened and restored. Into this green pasture our Lord God
gathers His sheep, feeds them in it with precious grass,
and restores them with fresh water. That is, He commits
to the holy Christian church the office of a shepherd, en-
trusts and gives to it the holy gospel and the sacraments,
so that by means of these it may care for and watch over
His sheep and so that these sheep may be richly provided with instruction, comfort, strength, and protection
against all evil. But those who preach the law of Moses
or the ordinances of men do not feed the sheep in a green
pasture but in the desert, where they famish, and lead
them to foul, smelly water, which will cause them to de-
cay and die.

By means of the allegory of the green pasture, however, the prophet wants to indicate the great abundance
and the riches of the holy gospel and of the knowledge of
Christ among the believers. For just as the grass in a
green pasture stands very thick and full and grows more
and more, so it is with the believers: they not only have
God's Word richly, but the more they use and apply it,
the more it increases and grows among them. Therefore,
the psalmist expresses himself very plainly. He does not
say, "He leads me once, or often, in a green pasture,"
but, "He leads me in them without ceasing, so that amid
the grass and in the pasture I may lie, rest, and dwell
securely and never suffer hunger or any other want."
The word that he uses here means "lie" and "rest," as a
four-footed animal lies and rests. In the same manner
Solomon also speaks in the seventy-second psalm, where
he prophesies that the kingdom of God and the gospel

will prevail with might and go to all places, and says, "In the land, on the tops of the mountains, may the grain wave and blossom forth in the cities like the grass of the field" (Ps. 72:16). David shows that he is speaking of the gospel also in this psalm when he says later, "He restores my soul"; and "Thy rod and Thy staff, they comfort me."

This then, is the first fruit of the dear Word: that the Christians are instructed through it in such a way that they grow in faith and hope, learn to commit all their doings and ways unto God, and hope in Him for everything they need in soul and body.

He leads me to the fresh water.

This is the second fruit of the dear Word. It is not only the believers' pasture and grass, with which they are satisfied and grow strong in the faith; to them it is also pleasantly cool, fresh water, through which they gain refreshment and comfort. The psalmist therefore does not stop with saying, "He makes me lie down in green pastures," but also adds, "He leads me to the fresh water." It is as though he would say, "In great heat, when the sun smites hard (Ps. 121:6) and I can have no shade, He leads me to fresh water, gives me to drink, and refreshes me." That is, in all kinds of afflictions, anxieties, and distresses—spiritual and physical—when I cannot find help and comfort anywhere, I cling to the Word of grace. There alone, and nowhere else, do I find the right comfort and refreshment, and find it richly. What he says here in figurative language he expresses elsewhere in sober, clear words and says, "If Thy Law had not been my delight, I should have perished in my affliction. I will never forget it, for with it Thou doest restore me" (Ps. 119:92).

45

But he still retains the metaphor of the shepherd and the sheep, which is a common thing among all the prophets. For the Jews had their best food from sheep and other animals and commonly were shepherds, even as David himself and also the dear patriarchs were shepherds. Therefore this metaphor is often employed in Scripture. David, however, speaks of this matter in keeping with the nature of the country; the Promised Land is a hot, dry, sandy, stony land that has many deserts and little water. Therefore the book of Genesis reports more than once how the shepherds of the heathen quarreled with the shepherds of the patriarchs about water.[1] They accordingly considered it a special treasure in that land when they could have water for their cattle. In our countries this is unknown, for there is enough water everywhere. David has looked at his land and cites it as a special blessing that he is under the protection of the Lord, who not only feeds him in a green pasture but during the heat also leads him to the fresh water.

In brief, he wishes to say this: as little as one can come to the knowledge of God and the truth and to the right faith without the Word of God, just so little can one find comfort and peace of conscience without it. The world has its comfort and joy, too, but these last only a moment; when anxiety and distress and especially the last hour comes, then it is as Solomon says, "After laughter the heart is sad; and after joy comes grief" (Prov. 14:13). But those who drink of this fresh and living water may indeed suffer affliction and distress in the world, but they will never lack genuine comfort. Especially when the moment of crisis comes, the page turns for them to the place where it says, "After brief weeping comes eter-

---

[1]Cf. Gen. 21:25, 26:19–22.

nal laughter; after a small sorrow comes glorious joy" (2 Cor. 4:17). For they shall not weep and be sorrowful both here and there, but it will be as Christ says, "Blessed are you that weep here, for you shall laugh" (Luke 6:21).

He restores my soul, He leads me in the right path for His name's sake.

Here the prophet himself explains what kind of pasture and fresh water he has been discussing, namely, that kind by which the soul is strengthened and restored. That, however, can be nothing else than God's Word. But because our Lord God has a twofold Word, the law and the gospel, the prophet makes it sufficiently clear that he is speaking here not of the law but of the gospel when he says, "He restores my soul." The law cannot restore the soul, for it is a Word that makes demands on us and commands us that we shall love God with all our hearts and our neighbors as ourselves (Matt. 22:37, 39). It damns him that does otherwise and pronounces this sentence upon him, "Cursed be everyone who does not do all the things written in the Book of the Law" (Gal. 3:10; Deut. 27:26). Now, it is certain that nobody on earth does that; therefore, the law comes in due time with its sentence and only grieves and frightens the souls. Where no help is provided, it presses them so that they must despair and be lost forever. Saint Paul therefore says, "By the law comes only knowledge of sin" (Rom. 3:20), and, "The law brings only wrath" (Rom. 4:15).

The gospel, however, is a blessed Word. It demands nothing of us, but announces everything that is good, namely, that God has given us poor sinners His only Son and that He is to be our Shepherd. He will seek us famished and scattered sheep and give His life for us, to redeem us from sin, from eternal death, and from the power of the devil. That is the green grass and the fresh water with which the Lord restores our souls. Thus we are rid of our bad consciences and sad thoughts. More of that in the fourth verse.

He leads me in the right path.

"The Lord," he says, "does not stop with feeding me in a green pasture and leading me to the fresh water and thus restoring my soul. He also leads me in the right paths so that I may not go astray, get into the wilderness, and thus perish. That is, He keeps me in pure doctrine, that I may not be misled by false spirits nor fall away from it because of temptation or offense; that I may know how I am to walk and live outwardly and not take offense at the holiness and the strict lives of hypocrites; and that I may also know what is the right doctrine, faith, and worship."

Another fine fruit and power of the dear Word is this: those who cling to it firmly not only receive from it strength and comfort for their souls, but are also protected against false doctrine and false holiness. Many, it is true, receive this treasure but without being able to keep it. For when a man becomes smug and presumptuous and thinks he is safe, he will soon be lost; before he can look about, he has been led astray. The devil can also assume holiness and disguise himself, as Saint Paul says, as "an angel of light" (2 Cor. 11:14). His servants, then, pretend to be preachers of righteousness and enter the flock of Christ in sheep's clothing but inwardly are ravenous wolves (Matt. 7:15). Therefore, we should watch and pray, as the prophet does in the last verse, that our Shepherd would keep us true to the treasure He has given us. Those who fail in this surely lose the treasure, and, as Christ says, their last state becomes worse than the first (Luke 11:26). For later they become the most venomous foes of Christianity and do much more harm with their false doctrine than the tyrants do with the sword. Saint Paul indeed learned this from the false prophets who led his Corinthians and Galatians astray for a time and later carried off all of Asia (2 Tim. 1:15). In our days we see this, too, in the Anabaptists and other schismatic spirits.

For His name's sake.

The name of God is the preaching of God, by which He is glorified and made known as the gracious, merciful, patient, truthful, and faithful one. Although we are the children of wrath (Eph. 2:3) and are guilty of eternal death, He forgives us all our sins and receives us as His children and heirs. That is His name, and that name He causes to be proclaimed through the Word. He wants to be known, glorified, and honored by these means; and, according to the first commandment, He will also reveal Himself to us exactly as He has men preach of Him (Exod. 20:5, 6). Thus, without ceasing, He strengthens and restores our souls spiritually and keeps us from falling into error, and also feeds us bodily and wards off all misfortune. But only those who cling to His Word, and who believe and confess boldly that all the gifts and possessions of body and soul that they own, they have received from God purely out of grace and kindness, that is, solely for His name's sake and not because of their own deeds and merits—only they give Him the honor of being exactly as we have just been told. They thank Him for His blessings and also proclaim these blessings to others. No haughty saints, such as heretics, schismatic spirits, or enemies and blasphemers of the Word of God, can give Him this honor, for they glorify not His name but their own.

Even though I walk through the valley of the shadow, I fear no evil; for Thou art with me; Thy rod and Thy staff, they comfort me.

Until now the prophet has shown that those who have and love God's Word do not want, for the Lord is their Shepherd. This Shepherd not only feeds them in a green pasture and leads them to the fresh water so that they may become quite fat and strong and restored spiritually and physically; He also keeps them from becoming weary of the good pasture and the fresh water, and from leaving the green pasture and straying from the right path into the desert. That is the first part of this psalm. Now he goes on to teach that those who are this Lord's sheep are surrounded by much danger and misfortune. But the Lord, he says, not only protects them but also saves them from all temptations and distresses, for He is with them. He also shows beautifully in what way He is with them.

Here you can see that as soon as the Word is preached and as soon as there are people that accept and confess it, the devil quickly appears with all his angels and arouses the world with all its might against this Word, to stifle it and completely destroy those that have and confess it. Whatever our Lord God says or does must be swept clean and pass through the fire. It is very important for Christians to know this, else they may become perplexed and think, "How can this be harmonized? The prophet has said above, 'The Lord is my Shepherd, I shall not want,' and here he says the very opposite: that he must walk through the valley of the shadow. And in the following verse he admits that he has enemies. With these words he surely lets us know well enough that he does want—too much, yes, practically everything. For he who has enemies and wanders through the valley of the shadow can see no light, that is, he has neither comfort nor hope but is forsaken by everybody. Everything is black and dark before his eyes, even the beautiful, bright sun. How, then, can it be true that he does not want?"

Here you must not be guided by your eyes or follow your reason, as the world does. The world cannot see this rich, splendid comfort of the Christians, that they want nothing. Yes, the world considers it quite certain that the opposite is true, namely, that on earth there are no poorer, more miserable, and more unhappy people than these same Christians. And [the world] helps very faithfully and boldly in having them most cruelly persecuted, exiled, reviled, and killed. And when the world does this, it thinks that thereby it has offered service to God (John 16:2). Outwardly, then, it appears as if the Christians were the scattered sheep, forsaken by God and surrendered to the very jaws of the wolves, and that they wanted absolutely everything.

But those who serve the great god mammon or belly appear to the world to be the dear sheep which do not want and which, as the psalm says, God richly supports, comforts, and guards against all danger and misfortune. For they have what their hearts desire: honor, possessions, joy, pleasure, and everyone's favor. Nor do they have to fear that because of their faith they will be persecuted and killed. As long as they do not believe in Christ or confess Him, the only true Shepherd, they believe in the devil and his mother.[2] Otherwise, too, they do as they will, for example, in covetousness. Not only do they prosper therein, but they also appear to be living saints, who are holding fast to the old faith and are not misled by any such heresy as this, that, as David teaches here, the Lord alone is a Shepherd. It is so horrible, great, and deadly a sin to believe in this shepherd[3] and to confess him that there has never been anything on earth like it. Even his Holiness the Pope, who otherwise grants dispensation from all sins and even forgives them, is unable to grant forgiveness in the case of this sin only.

Therefore, I say, do not follow the world in this matter, nor your reason which, because it judges according to outward appearances, becomes a fool and considers the prophet a liar for saying, "I shall not want." You, however, cling to God's Word and promise, as was also said before. Listen to your Shepherd, however, and whatever He speaks to you. Judge according to His voice and not according to what your eyes see and your heart feels. Then you have gained the victory. That is how the prophet acts in his own case. He confesses that he is walking through the valley of the shadow, that is, that he is surrounded by distresses, sadness, anxiety, and trouble, as can also be seen from his life's history and from other psalms. His need of comfort is indicated sufficiently by the fact that he is grieved and has enemies. Nevertheless, he says, "Though my temptations were even more numerous and great, and though my lot were even worse, and though I were already in the jaws of death, yet I will fear no evil. Not that I could assist my-

---

[2]This is perhaps a variation on Luther's more customary metaphor of the world as the devil's bride.

[3]Either Luther is speaking ironically here, or by the term "shepherd" he means the devil.

self through my own care, efforts, work, or help. Nor do I depend on my own wisdom, piety, royal power, or riches. Here all human help, counsel, comfort, and power are far too weak. This, however, avails for me, that the Lord is with me."

It is as if he would say, "As for me, I am indeed weak, sad, anxious, and surrounded by all kinds of danger and misfortune. Because of my sin, my heart and my conscience are not satisfied either. I experience such horrible terrors of death and hell that I almost despair. Yet though the whole world and also the gates of hell should oppose me, that will not dismay me (Matt. 16:18). Yes, I will not be afraid of all the evil and sorrow that they may be able to lay on me, for the Lord is with me. The Lord is my counselor, comforter, protector, and helper—the Lord, I say, who has created heaven and earth and everything that is in it out of a more trifling thing than a speck of dust, that is, out of nothing. To Him all creation is subject: angels, devils, men, sin, death. In brief, He has everything in His power. And therefore I fear no evil."

Asaph also speaks thus in the seventy-third psalm. There he comforts the Christians because of the great offense that the wicked prosper so greatly on earth, while the dear saints of God are constantly tormented, and says, "If only I have Thee, Lord, I will ask nothing of heaven and earth. Even though my body and soul should fail, Thou, O God, art the strength of my heart and my portion forever" (Ps. 73:23). But how the Lord is with him, he now goes on to show, and says,

Thy rod and Thy staff, they comfort me.

"The Lord," he says, "is with me, but not bodily so that I might see or hear Him. This presence of the Lord of which I am speaking is not to be grasped by the five senses. But faith sees it and believes surely that the Lord is nearer to us than we are to ourselves." How? Through His Word. He says therefore, "Thy rod and Thy staff, they comfort me." It is as though he would say, "In all of my anxieties and troubles I find nothing on earth that might help to satisfy me. But then God's Word is my rod and my staff. To that Word I will cling, and by it I raise myself up again. I will also learn for sure that the Lord is with me and that He not only strengthens and comforts me with this same Word in all distresses and temptations, but that He also redeems me from all my enemies, contrary to the will of the devil and the world."

With the words, "Thy rod and Thy staff, they comfort me," he returns to the metaphor of the shepherd and the sheep. He would speak thus, "Even as a bodily shepherd guides his sheep with his rod or staff and leads them to fresh water where they find food and drink and protects them with his staff against all danger, so the Lord, the real Shepherd, leads and guides me also with His staff, that is, with His Word, so that I may walk before Him with a good faith and a happy conscience, remain in the right path, and be able to protect myself against false doctrine and fictitious holiness. He also protects me against all danger and evil of spirit and of body and saves me from all my enemies with His staff. That is, with the same Word He strengthens and comforts me so richly that no evil can be so great, be it of spirit or body, that I cannot endure and overcome it."

You see, then, that the prophet is not speaking here of any human help, protection, and comfort. He does not draw a sword. Everything is done here in a hidden and mysterious manner through the Word, so that no one becomes aware of any protection and comfort but the believers alone. Here David lays down a common rule for all Christians, and it is to be well noted: that there is no other way or counsel on earth to get rid of all kinds of temptation than this, that a man cast all his cares upon God, take Him at His Word of grace, hold fast to it, and not let it be taken from him in any way. Whoever does that can be satisfied, whether he prospers or fails, whether he lives or dies. And in the end he can also stand and must succeed against all devils, the world, and evil. That is the way, I feel, to magnify the dear Word and to credit it with much greater power than the power of all angels and men. And that is the way in which also Saint Paul magnifies it, "The gospel," he says, "is a power of God that saves all who believe in it" (Rom. 1:16).

Here the prophet also touches upon the office of preaching. For through the oral preaching of the Word, which enters the ears and touches the heart by faith, and through the holy sacraments our Lord God accomplished all these things in His Christendom, namely, that men are brought to faith, are strengthened in faith, are kept in pure doctrine, and in the end are enabled to withstand all the assaults of the devil and the world. Without these means, Word and sacrament, we obtain none of these things. For since the beginning of the world God has dealt with all the saints through His Word and, in addition, has given them external signs of grace. This I say so that no one may venture to deal with God without these means or build for himself a special way to heaven, lest he fall and break his neck, as the pope has done to his followers and still does, and as today the Anabaptists and other schismatic spirits do.

But with the words "Thy rod and Thy staff, they comfort me," the prophet wishes to say something special. It is as though he would say, "Moses is also a shepherd and also has a rod and a staff. But he does nothing with them but drive and plague and burden his sheep with an unbearable burden (Acts 15:10, Isa. 9:3). Therefore, he is a terrible, horrible shepherd, whom the sheep only fear and from whom they flee. But Thou, O Lord, do not drive and frighten Thy sheep with Thy rod and Thy staff, nor burden them, but only comfort them."

Therefore, he is speaking here about the office of preaching in the New Testament, which proclaims to the world that "Christ came into the world to save sinners" (1 Tim. 1:15) and that He has gained this salvation for sinners by giving His life for them. Whoever believes this should not perish but have eternal life (John 3:16). That is the rod and the staff by which the souls obtain rest, comfort, and joy. In spiritual shepherding, that is, in the kingdom of Christ, one should, therefore, preach to the sheep of Christ—the goats one must govern with Moses and the emperor's rod and staff—not the law of God, much less the ordinances of men, but the gospel, which the prophet with metaphorical words calls a rod of comfort and a staff of comfort. For through the gospel, Christ's sheep obtain strength in their faith, rest in their hearts, and comfort in all kinds of anxieties and perils of death.

Those who preach this way conduct the office of a spiritual shepherd properly, feed the sheep of Christ in a green pasture, lead them to the fresh water, restore their souls, keep them from being led astray, and comfort them with Christ's rod and staff. Where men hear such preachers, they should believe for certain that they are hearing Christ Himself. They should also acknowledge such preachers as right shepherds, that is, as servants of Christ and stewards of God (1 Cor. 4:1), and pay no attention at all to the fact that the world proclaims and damns them as heretics and seducers. Those who preach something else than the gospel, who guide men to works, merit, and self-appointed holiness, may indeed praise themselves ten times over as the followers of the apostles, adorn themselves with the name and title of the Christian Church, and even raise the dead. Actually they are horrible wolves and murderers that do not spare the flock of Christ, but scatter, torture, and slaughter it not only spiritually but also bodily, as is now clearly and plainly to be seen.

Earlier the prophet called God's Word, or the Gospel, grass, water, the right path, a rod, a staff. In the fifth verse he calls it a table that is prepared for us, an oil, and a cup that is filled to overflowing. He takes these metaphors of the table, oil, and cup from the Jews' Old Testament worship of God, and says practically the same thing he had said before—namely, that those who have God's Word are richly supplied with all things of body and soul—except that here he indicates these blessings with other figures and allegories. First he presents the picture of the table on which the showbread had to be set at all times (Exod. 25:30; 40:23). And he also shows what that means, and says:

Thou preparest a table before me against my enemies; Thou anointest my head with oil, Thou pourest my cup full.

Here the prophet confesses frankly that he has enemies. He says, however, that he defends himself against them and drives them back in this way, that the Lord has prepared a table before him against these same enemies of his. Is not that a wonderful protector? I should think He would prepare before him a mighty wall, a strong rampart, a deep moat, an armor, and other arms and weapons that have to do with battle, through which he might be safe from his enemies or put them to flight. But He prepares a table before him, at which he is to eat and to drink and in this way to defeat his enemies. I, too, would like to wage war if, without any danger, care, trouble, and work, one could conquer one's enemies by doing nothing more than sitting at a table and eating, drinking, and making merry.

By means of these words, "Thou preparest a table before me in the presence of my enemies," the prophet wishes to indicate the great, splendid, and wonderful power of the dear Word. It is as though he would say, "Thou, O Lord, dost offer me so many good things and feed me so splendidly and richly at the table that Thou hast prepared for me. That is, Thou dost overwhelm me so greatly with the boundless knowledge of Thy dear Word, that through this Word I not only have rich comfort inwardly, in my heart, despite my guilty conscience, despite sin, fear, the terror of death, and God's wrath and judgment; through it I also become outwardly so courageous and invincible a hero that all my enemies cannot prevail against me. The more raging and raving and insane they are toward me, the less I worry about them; yes, instead, I am secure, happy, and cheerful. And that is true only because I have Thy Word. It gives me such strength and comfort in the presence of all my enemies, so that even when they rage and rave most violently, I feel more at ease than when I am sitting at a table and have all that my heart desires: food, drink, joy, pleasures, music, and the like."

Here you shall hear how highly blessed David exalts and praises the dear Word, namely, by telling us that by means of it the believers gain the victory over the devil, the world, the flesh, sin, conscience, and death. When one has the Word and in faith clings to it firmly, these enemies, who otherwise are invincible, must all yield and let themselves be taken captive. It is, however, a wonderful victory and power, also a very proud and haughty boast on the part of the believers, that they may compel and conquer all of these horrible and, as it were, almighty enemies, not by raging, biting, resisting, striking back, avenging, seeking counsel and help here and there, but by eating, drinking, rejoicing, sitting, being happy, and resting. All of this, as we have said, is accomplished through the Word. For in Scripture "eating and drinking" means believing and clinging firmly to the Word, and from this proceed peace, joy, comfort, strength, and the like.

Reason cannot accommodate itself to this wonderful victory of the believers. Here everything happens in a contradictory way. The world always persecutes and murders the Christians as the most harmful people on earth. When reason sees that, it must think that the Christians are succumbing and their enemies are supreme and victorious. Thus the Jews dealt with Christ, the apostles, and the believers, and executed them. When they had murdered, or at least exiled them, they cried, "On to victory! Those who have done us harm no longer can confound us. Now we shall act according to our own pleasure." But when they felt most secure, our Lord sent the Romans against them, who treated them so horribly that it frightens one to hear it. Several hundred and more years later He also gave the Romans their reward, who had killed many thousands of martyrs throughout the Roman Empire. He had the city of Rome conquered by the Goths and Wends four times within a few years, and finally had it burned down and leveled, and let the empire perish. Who was victorious now? The Jews and the Romans, who had shed the blood of the dear saints like water? Or the poor Christians, who had been killed like sheep led to the slaughter, and had no other defense and weapons than the dear Word?

David is not speaking here only about his own person, but by means of these words he shows how the holy Christian church fares. He gives it the proper coloration and paints a fine picture of it. Before God it is a pleasant green meadow, on which there is grass and water in abundance. That is, it is God's paradise and pleasure garden, adorned with all His gifts, and it has His inexpressible treasure: the holy sacraments and the dear Word, with which [He] instructs, governs, restores, and comforts His flock. To the world, however, it has a different appearance. It is a black, gloomy valley where neither joy nor pleasure is to be seen, but only distress, anxiety, and trouble. The devil assails it with all his might because of its treasure. Inwardly he tortures it with his venomous, fiery arrows (Eph. 6:16); outwardly he separates it with schisms and offenses (Rom. 16:17). And he also incites his bride, the world,[4] against it, which imposes upon it all misery and heartache through persecution, slander, blasphemy, damnation, and murder. It would not be surprising, therefore, if the dear Christian church were completely destroyed in a moment's time through the great craft and might of both the devil and the world. For it cannot defend itself against its enemies; they are much too strong, crafty, and powerful for it. So it is, as the prophet depicts it here, an innocent, simple, defenseless lamb, which neither will nor can do anyone any harm, but at all times is ready not only to do good but to receive evil in return.

How, then, does it happen that Christendom, which is

---

[4]A favorite metaphor of Luther's for the world.

so weak, can withstand the craft and the tyranny of the devil and the world? The Lord is its Shepherd; therefore, it does not want. He feeds and restores it spiritually and physically. He keeps it in the right path. He also gives it His rod and His staff as a sword. [The church] does not, however, wield this sword with its hand but with its mouth. With it, it not only comforts the sad but also puts the devil and all his apostles to flight, no matter how craftily and shrewdly they may defend themselves. Moreover, the Lord has prepared a table or paschal lamb before it, in order to destroy its enemies completely when they rage greatly, gnash their teeth against it, became mad, insane, raging, and raving, and call to their aid all their craft, strength, and power. Thus the dear bride of Christ can sit down at the table of her Lord, eat of the paschal lamb, drink of the fresh water, be happy and sing, "The Lord is my Shepherd, I shall not want." These are her weapons and guns, with which she has defeated and conquered all her foes until now. With these she will also retain the victory until Judgment Day. The more the devil and the world plague and torture her, the better she fares. For her betterment and growth come in persecution, suffering, and dying. Therefore, one of the old fathers has said, "The blood of the martyrs is a seed."[5] Where one is executed, a hundred others rise again. Of this wonderful victory several psalms sing; for example, the ninth, the tenth, and others.

In this way I also have been preserved by the grace of God [for] the past eighteen years. I have let my enemies rage, threaten, slander, and damn me, take counsel against me without ceasing, invent many evil devices, and practice many a piece of knavery. I have let them

---

[5]An allusion to Tertullian, *Apologeticus*, 50, which had become proverbial.

worry anxiously how they might kill me and destroy my teaching, or rather God's. Moreover, I have been happy and of good cheer—at one time better than at another—have not worried greatly about their raving and raging, but have clung to the staff of comfort and found my way to the Lord's table. That is, I have committed my cares to our Lord God, into which He had led me absolutely without my will or counsel; and meanwhile I spoke an Our Father or a psalm. That is all of the armor with which until now I have not only held off all my enemies, but by the grace of God have also accomplished so much that, when I look behind me and consider how matters stand in the papacy, I really must be surprised that things have gone so far. I should never have dared to imagine that even one tenth of what is now evident would happen. He that has begun the good work will also bring it to completion (Phil. 1:6), even though nine more hells and worlds were gathered together in a heap. Therefore, let every Christian thoroughly learn this art: to cling to this rod and this staff and to find his way to this table when sorrow or other misfortune appears. Then he will surely gain strength and comfort for everything that worries him.

The second metaphor is that of the oil, which is often employed in Holy Writ. It was, however, a precious oil, such as a balsam or other sweet-smelling liquid. The priests and the kings were customarily anointed with it. Furthermore, when the Jews had their festivals and wished to be happy, they would anoint or sprinkle themselves with such precious oil, as Jesus also mentions when He says, "When you fast, anoint your head, and wash your face" (Matt. 6:17). This custom, then, of using oil was common among these people when they wanted to be merry and happy (John 12:3). Magdalene also wished to make the Lord happy when she poured precious ointment of pure perfume on His head, for she saw that He was sad (Luke 7:38). The third metaphor is that of a cup, which they used in their worship when they brought drink offerings and rejoiced before the Lord.

With these words, "Thou anointest my head with oil, Thou pourest my cup full," the prophet, then, wishes to indicate the great, rich comfort that the believers have through the Word, that their consciences are sure, happy, and well satisfied amid all temptations and distresses, even death. It is as though he would say, "The Lord indeed makes an unusual warrior of me and arms me quite wonderfully against my enemies. I thought that He would have put armor on me, placed a helmet on my head, put a sword into my hand, and warned me to be cautious and give careful attention to the business at hand lest I be surprised by my enemies. But instead He places me at a table and prepares a splendid meal for me, anoints my head with precious balm or (after the fashion of our country) puts a wreath on my head as if, instead of going out to do battle, I were on my way to a party or a dance. And so that I may not want anything now, He fills my cup to overflowing so that at once I may drink, be happy and of good cheer, and get drunk. The prepared table, accordingly, is my armor, the precious balm my helmet, the overflowing cup my sword; and with these I shall conquer all my enemies." But is that not a wonderful armor and an even more wonderful victory?

David wishes to say, "Lord, Thy guests who are sitting at Thy table, the believers, not only become strong and bold giants in the presence of all their enemies, but they also become happy and drunk. That is due to the fact that Thou dost treat them well, as a rich man usually treats his guests. Thou dost feed them splendidly, make them happy and gay, and serve them so well with wine that they get drunk." All of that is done through the Word of grace. Through it the Lord, our Shepherd, feeds and strengthens the hearts of His believers, so that they defy all of their enemies and say with the prophet, "I am not afraid of the many hundreds of thousands of people who have set themselves against me round about" (Ps. 3:6). And above, in the fourth verse, he said, "I fear no evil; for Thou, Lord, art with me." He accordingly gives them the Holy Spirit together with the Word, yes, through this same Word. The Holy Spirit makes them not only courageous and bold, but also so secure and happy that they get drunk with a great and boundless joy.

David is thus speaking here of spiritual power, joy, and intoxication—the power of God (Rom. 1:16); and a joy in the Holy Spirit, as Saint Paul calls it (Rom. 14:17); and a blessed intoxication, in which the people are filled not with wine, for that is debauchery, but with the Holy Spirit (Eph. 5:18). And this is the armor and the weapons with which our Lord God equips His believers against the devil and the world; that is, He puts the Word into their mouths and puts courage, that is, the Holy Spirit, into their hearts. Unafraid and cheerful, they attack all their enemies with that equipment. They smite and conquer them despite all their [enemies'] power, wisdom, and holiness. Such warriors were the apostles on the day of Pentecost (Acts 2:1 ff). They stood up in Jerusalem against the command of the emperor and the high priest and acted as though they were veritable gods and all the others mere locusts. And they pressed forward with all strength and joy, as though they were intoxicated, as some actually mocked them and said they were filled with new wine. But Saint Peter showed from the prophet Joel that they were not filled with wine but with the Holy Spirit. Afterward he flayed about with his sword; that is, he opened his mouth and preached, and with one stroke he rescued three thousand souls from the devil.

But such power, joy, and blissful intoxication are manifested in the believers not only when they prosper and have peace, but also when they suffer and die. When the council at Jerusalem, therefore, had the apostles flogged, they rejoiced that they had been counted worthy to suffer dishonor for the name of Christ (Acts 5:41). And in Romans 5:3 Saint Paul says, "We also rejoice in our sufferings." Later on many martyrs, men and women went to their deaths with happy hearts and laughing mouths as though they were going to a happy festival or dance. So we read of Saint Agnes and Saint Agatha,[6] who were virgins of thirteen or fourteen years, and of many others. They not only boldly and confidently conquered the devil and the world through their deaths, but were also cheerful with all their hearts, just as if they had been drunk with great joy. And it does vex the devil beyond measure when one can so confidently despise his great might and guile. In our times, too, many have died cheerfully because they have confessed Christ. Similarly, we learn that many die in their beds with a fine understanding and faith and say with Simeon, "With peace and joy I now depart," so that it is a pleasure to behold, as I myself have often beheld it. And all this because, as the prophet says, they are anointed with the oil which the psalm calls an oil of gladness (Ps. 45:7), and

---

[6]Luther seems to be thinking primarily of Saint Agnes here, combining with the details of her martyrdom the story of another virgin martyr, Saint Agatha.

have drunk from the overflowing cup which the Lord has filled.

"Good!" you say, "but I do not yet find myself sufficiently well equipped to die cheerfully." That does not matter. As mentioned earlier, David did not always have the ability either; indeed, at times he complained that he had been cast away from the presence of God. Nor did other saints at all times have full confidence in God and an eternal pleasure and patience in their distresses and afflictions. Saint Paul at times trusted so securely and surely in Christ that he would not have bothered even to stand up because of the law, sin, death, and the devil. "It is no longer I who live," he says, "but Christ who lives in me" (Gal. 2:20). And, "My desire is to depart and to be with Christ" (Phil. 1:23). And, "Who shall separate us from the love of God? He did not spare His own Son, but gave Him up for us all. Will He not also give us all things with Him? Shall tribulation, or distress, or persecution, or the sword separate us from Him?" (Rom. 8:32, 35). When he speaks here of death, the devil, and all misfortune, he is as sure as though he were the strongest and greatest saint, for whom death would be pure joy. Elsewhere, then, he speaks as though he were the weakest and greatest sinner on earth. 1 Corinthians 2:3: "I was with you in weakness and in much fear and trembling." Romans 7:14: "I am carnal, sold under sin," which brings me into captivity. Romans 7:24: "Wretched man that I am! Who will deliver me from the body of this death?" And in Galatians 5:17, he teaches that in the saints there is an eternal struggle of the flesh against the spirit. Therefore, you ought not despair so soon, though you find yourself weak and fainthearted, but pray diligently that you might remain with the Word and grow in the faith and knowledge of Christ. This is what the prophet is doing here, teaching others to do by saying:

Goodness and mercy shall follow me all the days of my life; and I shall dwell in the house of the Lord forever.

Because the devil never stops tormenting the believers—inwardly with terror, outwardly with the wiles of false teachers and the power of the tyrants—the prophet here at the end earnestly asks that God, who has given him this treasure, would also keep him in it to the end. He says, "Oh, may the dear God grant His grace that goodness and mercy might follow me all the days of my life and that He might soon make manifest what He calls goodness and mercy," that is, that he might dwell in the house of the Lord forever. It is as though he would say, "Lord, Thou hast begun the matter. Thou hast given me Thy holy Word and received me among those who are Thy people, who know Thee, praise and magnify Thee. Continue to give Thy grace, that I may remain with the Word and nevermore be separated from Thy holy Christendom." Thus, he also prays in the twenty-seventh psalm, "One thing I ask of the Lord," he says, "that will I seek after; that I may dwell in the house of the Lord all the days of my life, to behold the beautiful worship of the Lord, and to visit His temple" (Ps. 27:4).

Thus, the prophet here teaches and admonishes all believers by his example not to become smug, proud, or presumptuous, but to fear and pray that they may not lose their treasure. Such an earnest admonition, however, should truly arouse us and awaken us to pray diligently. Blessed David, a prophet enlightened with all kinds of divine wisdom and knowledge and endowed with so many kinds of great and splendid gifts of God, prayed often and very earnestly that he might remain in possession of the blessings of God. We, then, who surely must be considered as nothing at all in comparison with David and who, besides, live at the end of the world—and that, as Christ and the apostles tell us, is a horrible and dangerous time—ought much more to awaken and to pray with all earnestness and diligence that we may remain in the house of the Lord all the days of our life, that is, that we may hear God's Word, through it receive the many kinds of blessings and fruits that were shown us above, and endure therein unto the end. May Christ, our only Shepherd and Savior, grant us this! Amen.

Isaiah's "suffering servant" chapter is one of the Old Testament's great Messianic prophecies. This prophecy was given hundreds of years before the birth of Jesus and was repeated as the Jews awaited the Messiah. It illustrates God's redemptive plan, describing the one who would come to suffer in the place of mankind. But Isaiah's message of the coming justification often fell on deaf ears.

Isaiah 53 describes the punishment of Christ in such detail that there was no excuse for the Jewish leaders, who were familiar with the Old Testament, to misinterpret his identity. Jesus himself made it clear that his mission was prophesied in the Old Testament and the Jewish leaders of his day should have understood who he was.

Luther spoke to Christians who were removed from the sufferings of Christ, who were perhaps unfamiliar with the prophecy. His recurring theme of faith as a gift of the Holy Spirit and of the Word is evident here.

CHAPTER THREE

Isaiah 53

Who has believed what we have heard?

Seeing the greatness of Christ, the prophet thinks of his fellow Jews, how few there will be to believe this. He had said that almost all would regard Him as an offense. Many Gentiles would receive Him but only a few Jews. For that reason he says here, "Who will ever believe this?" The Jews were indeed disgusted, as we see in the narratives of the Gospels and the Acts of the Apostles. This is what the prophet is bemoaning here, that so offensive an appearance of Christ must be received and respected by the kings. This reception takes place not by reason and its research facilities, but it is brought about solely by the Holy Spirit and the Word. To believe that Christ, so exceedingly disgraced and dying between robbers, is the Savior—this reason cannot believe. No more loathsome kind of death can be read about than that which Christ suffered, and to believe in Him under that form as the Messiah and to die in that faith—this is the office of the Holy Spirit. So far the prophet has completed one [verse] concerning Christ as the Servant hanging on the cross, and concerning His completely absurd appearance, and concerning His exalted kingdom, so that the kings will shut their mouths. Therefore I conclude that after His death, Christ will have an eternal kingdom.

He grew up like a young plant.

Here the prophet is still dealing with his prophecy concerning Christ's suffering. He grew up *like a young plant and like a root.* This is remarkable. *Before Him,* he says. Indeed, he grows up before God, but not in the eyes of the world. This is a metaphor, as if to say, a root does not grow in parched ground. It strikes me as if a lovely sprout were to grow up out of parched earth, that is, a dry Christ cannot possibly accomplish anything good. Trying to draw water from a rock and oil from iron is just as believable as saying that Christ must be splendid and glorious.

He had no form or comeliness. Not having form or comeliness means simply to deprive Him of everything, since no robber was completely without form. But here there is to be no form or adornment whatever.

We look at Him, because He was crucified publicly.

There was no beauty that we should desire Him. "There was nothing to attract us, nothing that we might care for. Everything about Him was repulsive." See how the prophet toils as he describes His contemptible appearance. It is as if he were saying, "The people treated Him in a most horrible way."

He was despised and rejected by men; a man of sorrows, and acquainted with grief.

For *rejected by men* the Hebrew has "one for whom there is no concern whatever; one from whom all turn away." This is not an easy suffering. These words cannot be understood as referring to the glory of the kingdom, nor do they speak of a simple and spiritual suffering. They speak rather of a physical, open, and extremely shameful suffering. Away with the Jews who refuse to admit that this refers to Christ! They imagine two Messiahs. They say that one has come already and is walking around in the world in the garb of a beggar and that a second one is to come in earthly glory. Thus this text compelled them.

A man of sorrows. This does not denote weaknesses but many sicknesses and griefs. He is a man wounded and beaten, as the following shows.

As one from whom men hide their faces.

Faces must be referred to others who saw Him; that is, as often as they saw Christ, they turned away from His wretched face. There was a revulsion of seeing. Here are two [verses] in which the prophet depicts both the glory of Christ and the lack of glory and His suffering. Now follows a third [verse] which shows what Christ would do.

We have heard that in these paragraphs there was a description of Christ's person with respect to His suffering and His glorification. This passage forms the basis for the Church's faith that Christ's kingdom is not of this world. Now follows what He would accomplish by His suffering, whether He suffered for His own sake or for the sake of others. And this is the second part of our understanding and justification, to know that Christ suffered and was cursed and killed, but FOR US. It is not enough to know the matter, the suffering, but it is necessary to know its function. The pope retained the matter but denied the function. The Anabaptists deny both.

Surely He has borne our griefs and carried our sorrows; yet we esteemed Him stricken, smitten by God, and afflicted.

This states the purpose of Christ's suffering. It was not for Himself and His own sins, but for our sins and griefs. He bore what we should have suffered. Here you see the fountain from which Saint Paul draws countless dreams of the suffering and merits of Christ, and he condemns all religions, merits, and endeavors in the whole world through which men seek salvation. Note the countless sects who to this day are toiling to obtain salvation. But here the prophet says, "He for us." It is difficult for the flesh to repudiate all its resources, to turn away from self, and to be carried over to Christ. It is for us who have merited nothing not to have regard for our merits but simply to cling to the Word between heaven and earth, even though we do not feel it. Unless we have been instructed by God, we will not understand this. Therefore I delight in this text as if it were a text of the New Testament. This new teaching which demolishes the righteousness of the law clearly appeared absurd to the Jews. For that reason the apostles needed Scripture, *Surely He has borne our griefs.* His suffering was nothing else than our sin. These words, OUR, US, FOR US, must be written in letters of gold. He who does not believe this is not a Christian. *Yet we esteemed Him [stricken].* We thought that He was suffering because of His own sin, as it were. In the eyes of the world and of the flesh, Christ does not suffer for us, since He seemed to have deserved it Himself. This is what the prophet says here too, that He was judged guilty in the eyes of the world. It is therefore difficult to believe that such a one suffered for us. The law is that everybody dies for his own sins. Natural reason, and divine as well, argues that everybody must bear his own sin. Yet He is struck down contrary to all law and custom. Hence, reason infers that He was smitten by God for His own sake. Therefore, the prophet leads us so earnestly beyond all righteousness and our rational capacity and confronts us with the suffering of Christ to impress upon us that all that Christ has is mine. This is the preaching of the whole gospel, to show us that Christ suffered for our sake contrary to law, right, and custom. He expounds more fully what His suffering for us means.

He was wounded.

The prophet is eloquent in describing the suffering of Christ. Word by word he expounds it in opposition to the hardened Jews. Do you want to know what it is to bear our sins, that is, what it means that *He was wounded?* Here you have Christ delineated perfectly and absolutely, since this chapter speaks of Him. Christ was a man, a servant of the Word, who by means of suffering bore our sins. What will the unrestrained Jew answer in opposition to this delineation? From this you must infer how far apart are the teachings of Paul and the pope. Paul clings to Christ alone as the sin bearer. By means of this one [name], "Lamb of God" (John 1:29), John the Baptist understands this levitical sacrifice, that He suffered for the sins of all. It follows, then, that the Law and merits do not justify. Away with the antichrist pope with his traditions, since Christ has borne all these things! I marvel that this text was so greatly obscured in the church. They note the concern of Scripture that faith without works is dead, and we say the same thing. In public argument, however, we say that works are indeed necessary, but not as justifying elements. Thus, anyone may privately come to the conclusion, "It is all the same whether I have sinned or whether I have done well." This is hard for the conscience to believe, that it is the same and in fact something angelic and divine. Therefore, this text draws the following conclusion: "Christ alone bears our sins. Our works are not Christ. Therefore, there is no righteousness of works." Surely none of the papists can escape this fact when he sees Scripture as a whole, that Christ has accomplished all things for justification and therefore we have not done it. Appeal to works, rewards, and merits and make much of them in the realm of outward recompense. Only do not make them responsible for justification and the forgiveness of sins. We can preach and uphold this passage in public, but we can only believe it with difficulty in private. If we preserve this article, "Jesus Christ is the Savior," all other articles concerning the Holy Spirit and of the church and of Scripture are safe. Thus Satan attacks no article so much as this one. He alone is a Christian who believes that Christ labors for us and that He is the Lamb of God slain for our sins. While this article stands, all the monasteries of righteousness are struck down by lightning. In the light of this text read all the epistles of Paul with regard to redemption, salvation, and liberation, because they are all drawn from this fountain. A blind papacy read and chanted these and similar words as in a dream, and no one really considered them. If they had, they would have cast off all righteousness from themselves. Hence, it is not enough to know and accept the fact. One must also accept the function and the power of the fact. If we have this, we stand unconquered on the royal road, and the Holy Spirit is present in the face of all sects and deceptions. When this doctrine is safe, we firmly stand up to all people, but where this article is lost, we proceed from one error to the next, as we observe in the babbling Enthusiasts and in Erasmus. Our nature is opposed to the function and power of Christ's Passion. As far as the fact itself is concerned, both the pope and the Turk believe it and proclaim it, but they do not accept its function. As for you, lift up this article and extol it above every law and righteousness, and let it be to you a measureless sea over against a little spark. The sea is Christ who has suffered. Your works and your righteousness are the little spark. Therefore, beware as you place your sins on your conscience that you do not panic, but freely place them on Christ, as this text says, "He has borne our iniquities." We must clearly transfer our sins from ourselves to Christ. If you want to regard your sin as resting on you, such a thought in your heart is not of God, but of Satan himself, contrary to Scripture, which by God's will places your sin on Christ. Hence, you must say, "I see my sin in Christ, therefore, my sin is not mine but another's. I see it in Christ." It is a great thing to say confidently, "My sin is not mine." However, it is a supreme conflict with a most powerful beast, which here becomes most powerful, "I behold sins heaped on Christ." Thus, a certain hermit who was extremely harassed by Satan could not evade him, but said, "I have not sinned. Everybody must look upon his conscience as free." He did not answer well because he did have sin. This is what he should have said, "My sins have been transferred to Christ; He has them." This is the grafting of the wild olive into the olive tree. It is not without purpose that the prophet uses so many words in this article, since it is necessary for a Christian to know that these are his own sins, whatever they are, and that they have been borne by Christ, by whom we have been redeemed and saved. This is the Savior from eternal damnation, from death, and from sin. So by this thunderbolt the law and its righteousness are struck down, as you see Paul treat this matter in detail.

Something further must be noted, [so that] those who do not feel this [assurance of salvation] despair. There Satan can turn the antidote into poison and the hope into despair. For when a Christian hears these supreme consolations and then sees how weak he is with regard to his faith in them, he soon thinks that they do not apply to him. In this way Satan can turn consolation into distress. But as for you, however weak you are, know that you are a Christian, whether you believe perfectly or imperfectly, even while weakness and a feeling of death and sin remain with you. To such a person we must say, "Brother, your situation is not desperate, but pray together with the apostles for the perfection of your faith." Paul also struggled with this problem and was deeply disturbed. A Christian is not yet perfect, but he is a Christian who has, that is, who begins to have, the righteousness of God. I say this for the sake of the weak, so that they will not despair when they feel the bite of sin within themselves. They should not yet be masters and doctors but disciples of Christ, people who learn Christ, not perfect teachers. Let it suffice for us to remain with that Word as learners. Therefore, however perfect and absolute the teaching of Christ is that affirms that all our sins belong to Christ, it is not perfect in our life. It is enough for us to have begun and to be in the state of reaching after what is before us. Hence, a Christian man must be especially vexed in his conscience and heart by Satan, and yet he must remain in the Word and not seek peace anywhere else than in Christ. We must not make a log or a rock out of the Christian as one who does not feel sin in himself. This is the claim of the exceedingly spiritual Enthusiasts.

The chastisement of peace. Peter treats this passage (1 Pet. 2:24). Christ is not so much a judge and an angry God but one who bears and carries our sins, a mediator. Away with the papists, who have set Christ before us as a terrible judge and have turned the saints into intercessors! There they have added fuel to the fire. By nature we are already afraid of God. Blessed therefore are those who as uncorrupted young people arrived at this understanding, that they can say, "I only knew Jesus Christ as the bearer of my sins." The name of Christ, then, is most agreeable. *The chastisement, or punishment, of our peace,* that is, His chastisement is the remedy that brings peace to our conscience. [Apart from] Christ there is nothing but disorder. But He was chastised for the sake of our peace. Note the wonderful exchange: one man sins, another pays the penalty; one deserves peace, the other has it. The one who should have peace has chastisement, while the one who should have chastisement has peace. It is a difficult thing to know what Christ is. Would that our Enthusiasts saw this clearly!

And with His stripes we are healed. See how delightfully the prophet sets Christ before us. It is a remarkable plaster. His stripes are our healing. The stripes should be ours and the healing in Christ. Hence this is what we must say to the Christian, "If you want to be healed, do not look at your own wounds, but fix your gaze on Christ."

All we like sheep have gone astray.

This is the conclusion and confutation of the preceding. There he calls all our labors and endeavors errors. Christ alone was without sin. In this text all the apostles have attacked the religions and the law itself. *All we have gone astray.* The religions through their own rules and their own way want to load our sins on us and say, "If you will observe these things, you will be free from your sins." Yet the prophet says that "our sins" and the sins "of all men" have been placed on Christ.

All we like sheep have gone astray. As I said [before], This is the supreme and chief article of faith, that our sins, placed on Christ, are not ours; again, that the peace is not Christ's but ours. Once this foundation is established, all will be well with the superstructure. If we do not bump against this rock, other teachings will not harm us. This article alone Satan cannot but attack by means of tyrants and sects. The whole world can put up with every sectarian teaching and even support it in peace. But it cannot bear this faith and the rejection of all works and merits. Because self-glory is brought to naught and the world likes to hear its own glory, it is not willing to reject its own. [Thus,] the head of self-righteousness must be lopped off. I grant that the works of the godly are good and right, but they do not justify. This Satan cannot bear, and because of this we are persecuted and we suffer to the present day, since we have taught all things in peace, tranquility, patience, and purity, certainly more than he. By this text we have cast down every foreign righteousness and hypocrisy. Therefore, write this text on the foundation in golden letters or in your own blood. That is why he says *all we*, and no one is excepted.

Each one of us all, because Christ has nothing from us but death and labor (cf. chapter 43) and we have righteousness and life from Him.

And the Lord has laid. This confirms our conscience that Christ did not take our sins by His own will but by the will of the Father who had mercy on us. *On Him*, not on us, contrary to every law and order, where whoever sins is punished. Here, however, we have the punishment of our sins on Christ Himself. In public life, however, if anyone sins openly, let him be punished by the magistrate.

He was offered because He Himself wanted it.

This is noted and sung everywhere against the scandal of the cross over against Jews and Gentiles who say, "How does He wish to save others when He could not save Himself?" (cf. Matt. 27:42). For that reason this text responds to this slander, *Because He Himself wanted it.* This is a good thought, but it is different in Hebrew. *He was oppressed, and He was afflicted, yet He opened not His mouth, like a lamb that is led to the slaughter.* That text about His suffering is treated by Peter in this way, "When He suffered, He did not threaten" (1 Pet. 2:23).

[Thus,] that [verse] expresses the will and the patience of Christ as He suffers, that He does not even think of vengeance. This is the way for Christians to suffer, that they endure very patiently without threats and curses, yea, that they pray for and bless their tormentors. Therefore, he depicts Christ's patience by comparing Him in a most felicitous way with a sheep. This is the force of that crucifixion, that such a Christ will suffer who is described as overflowing in suffering like that of sheep, with His whole heart filled with love.

Led to the slaughter. The sheep that is to be shorn and slaughtered is silent. So Christ, keeping silence, always sympathizes with their ills. Thus, you have Christ undergoing most shameful suffering in His person and yet suffering with a most patient heart. Having completed the first aspect, the prophet begins the second one, regarding the resurrection.

By oppression and judgment He was taken away.

Now he begins to treat His glorification. Behold, here he declares that He whom he had until now depicted as a sheep to be killed and whom he had described as destined for a most shameful death for the sins of others is to be raised again. Now he describes Him again. He is not dead but taken away from oppression. Here he says that His *oppression and judgment* is finished. This cannot be said of a dead person remaining in the grave, but it can be said of one liberated and revived. The text says that He was oppressed and in judgment but has now been removed from them, hence resurrected.

As for His generation, who will tell it? Who can relate its duration, since His life and duration is eternal? Note the two contrary statements: someone dying and yet enduring forever. *Generation* properly means age, era, a lifetime. It is a proverbial statement that "a generation goes, and a generation comes, but the earth remains forever" (Eccles. 1:4). This must be understood as referring not to generation but to age. Here, then, the prophet established Christ in an eternal age, something that cannot be expressed, namely, that He has been transposed into eternal life. Peter expounds this passage in Acts, where he says, "God raised Him up, having loosed the pangs of death, because it was not possible for Him to be held by it" (Acts 2:24), and led Him into generation, that is, into length of life and eternity. Christ has such length of life that it cannot be expressed. Unless we believe it by faith, eternity is beyond expression.

That He was cut off out of the land of the living, stricken for the transgression of My people. Again he says that Christ was stricken *for the transgression of My people.* Ever and again he says *for the sins of My people.* Let us not simply pass over Christ's suffering, but we must always look to its function, that it was for the sake of our sins. He says that He was separated and brought into another life, something no one understands from the perspective of this life. Therefore, the Jews are in error when they hope that He will reign in this life. No, in this life He served, preached, and suffered, and then He passed out of this world to another place.

From the land of the living, from this world where we live. Through this suffering He was transported from a mortal existence to an immortal one.

And they made His grave with the wicked.

If the Jews and we, in our weakness, should hitherto have been in doubt about the suffering Christ, the following proves it even more, as if to say, He not only died, but He was also buried. *His grave will be given Him with the ungodly and with a rich man in His death.* It is clearly evident that Christ was buried and dead. The Jews read "lifted up," not "buried." Here, however, the text clearly states that He was buried. No one is said to be buried unless he were dead, and so He was buried as an ungodly man. In this way this text refutes the slanders which deny that Christ died, and it is a strengthening of our faith.

Let us here look at the grammar. We are dealing with a Hebraism. In Scripture "rich man" is used instead of "ungodly" through a certain figure of speech. This is so since it often happens that the rich of this world are ungodly and their riches are often used for ungodly purposes. Therefore, he says here that He died like an ungodly man and was buried like a rich man, just as the gospel reports that He was put to death as a rebel and was buried with this name and disgrace attached to Him. The Jews, who might here dispute that Christ is king, cannot quibble, since He was to die in this way according to Scripture.

Although He had done no violence, and there was no deceit in His mouth. The most innocent Christ was judged by the Jews to be the most guilty, He who was most innocent and guiltless in His teaching and His life. They had not a word to say to Him. Although He was innocent, yet the Lord willed it that He should take upon Himself to be the most criminal of men. Therefore, he compares Him with all other men, and they, even though most holy, are guilty. This one Christ alone is the exception; He alone is righteous and holy. For that reason death could not hold Him.

If He gave His soul as the measure.

You now have the person suffering and a description of His death and resurrection. Now he describes the fruit of His Passion, and this is His fruit, that He will have His future kingdom according to the statement, "He sits at the right hand of the Father, from thence He shall come."[1] *If He gave His soul*, that is, He Himself gave His life as an offering for the transgression. "Transgression" is properly called "guilt" in Psalm 32:5. And they do not commit sin. "To commit sin" properly means that someone has done something and remains guilty. Thus, we are unable to remove our guilt. Therefore, only Christ can do it.

Since, therefore, *He gave His life for sin*, it follows that *He shall see His seed and His days shall be prolonged*. Thus, he wants to say, "We hope that the Messiah, of whom you say that He is dead, will be the completely unconquerable King." And we say to them, "He will be a king both ancient and eternal and will see His offspring for a very long time. None of your kings will forever and eternally see his offspring, as He will." A king of the world does not see his offspring for long. In fact, when he dies, he leaves them behind. Here you see what *the will of the Lord* is. He placed all our iniquities upon Him, freeing us from death and giving us eternal life. This is *the will of God*.

The travail of His soul.

So far he has especially talked about His soul being in toil, in misfortune. Hence, He must now receive His reward. *He shall see the fruit and be satisfied*. He shall have His delight in all things and have a full measure of pleasures. Everything will go just as He wants it.

By His knowledge He will justify. As to the manner in which the course of the kingdom will proceed, how will this King progress? This will be the manner: *by His knowledge*. This is a very lovely text. *By His knowledge*

---

[1] From the Apostles' Creed.

He will justify many, because He shall bear their iniquities. Those who confess that their sins have been borne by Him are the righteous. The definition of righteousness is wonderful. The sophists say that righteousness is the fixed will to render to each his own. Here he says that righteousness is the knowledge of Christ, who bears our iniquities. Therefore whoever will know and believe in Christ as bearing his sins will be righteous.

Many servants. Thus the Gospel is the means or vehicle by which the knowledge of God reaches us. Hence the kingdom of Christ does not consist in works or endeavors, since no rule and no law, not even the law of Moses, can lead us to that knowledge, but we arrive at it through the Gospel. A Christian cannot arrive at this knowledge by means of any laws, either moral or civil, but he must ascend to heaven by means of the Gospel. Therefore, he says here *by His knowledge.* There is no other plan or method of obtaining liberty than the knowledge of Christ. For that reason Peter and Paul are constantly saying that we must increase in this knowledge, since we can never be perfect in it (cf. 2 Pet. 3:18; Col. 1:10). The knowledge of Christ must be construed in a passive sense. It is that by which He is known, the proclamation of His suffering and death. You must therefore note this new definition of righteousness. Righteousness is the knowledge of Christ. What is Christ? He is the person who bears all our sins. These are unspeakable gifts and hidden and unutterable kinds of wisdom.

We have heard this outstanding passage *by His knowledge* and *iniquities.* I have said that the individual words must be pondered in supreme faith, and they must be read and considered with the most watchful eyes, so that it is not simply any kind of knowledge or understanding but a knowledge that justifies, in opposition to other kinds of knowledge. Thus, you see this remarkable definition of righteousness through the knowledge of God. It sounds ridiculous to call righteousness a speculative knowledge. Therefore, it is said in Jeremiah 9:24: "Let him who glories glory in this, that he understands and knows Me." Therefore, this knowledge is the formal and substantial righteousness of the Christians, that is, faith in Christ, which I obtain through the Word. The Word I receive through the intellect, but to assent to that Word is the work of the Holy Spirit. It is not the work of reason, which always seeks its own kinds of righteousness. The Word, however, sets forth another righteousness through the consideration and the promises of Scripture, which causes this faith to be accounted for righteousness. This is our glory to know for certain that our righteousness is divine in that God does not impute our sins. Therefore, our righteousness is nothing else than knowing God. Let the Christian who has been persuaded by these words cling firmly to them, and let him not be deceived by any pretense of works or by his own suffering, but rather let him say, "It is written that the knowledge of God is our righteousness, and therefore, no monk, no celibate, is justified."

And He shall bear their iniquities. Here he repeats, as it were, the foundation. To bring Christ, this is righteousness. Another part is, Who is Christ? He answers, "Christ is not a judge and tormentor and tyrant, as reason apart from the Word fashions Him, but He is the bearer of our iniquities." Yet He will become judge and tryant to those who refused to believe in Him. It is, however, the office of Christ to bear our sins. Hence, we must conclude from this text, "If Christ bears my iniquities, then I do not bear them." All teachings which say that our sins must be borne by us are ungodly. Thus, from such a text countless thunderbolts have come forward against an ungodly self-righteousness. So Paul by this article of justification struck down every kind of self-righteousness. Therefore, we must diligently observe this article. I see that there are many snorers treating this article. They are the ones who consider these words the way a man does who looks at his face in a mirror (as James says, 1:23 f). The moment they come upon another object or business, they are overwhelmed, and they forget the grace of God. For that reason you must most diligently consider this article and not allow yourself to be led astray by other teachings, occupations, or persecutions.

Therefore I will divide Him a portion with the great, and He shall divide the spoil with the strong.

Here he repeats as if by an exclamation. Since *He poured out His soul in death* and was not simply dead but *was numbered with the trangressors,* the prophet in these words repeats the suffering of Christ. Here he says, *He gave His life into death.* With that battering ram he strikes the stubbornness of the Jews, who do not want to hear about the Christ who dies but who look for a Christ who never dies. Here the prophet in a very simple and expressive way depicts the manner of His death. He says He will die and then points with the fingers, *He will be numbered with the transgressors,* as if to say, "You Jews want to acknowledge your Christ. He will appear in such a form that He will die the most despised kind of death in the midst of robbers." The Jews, who look for a glorious Christ before they will believe in a crucified one, did not want to see this text. This is the way it happens to us who are blind, although as for us, let us believe in the crucified One.

Yet He bore the sins of many. He has described the death. Now he delineates the force and power of His sufferings. He says, "He did not die in vain, but all promises of Scripture have been fulfilled, and all our sins have been taken away. No, He did not toil in vain by His death, but He died to fulfill the promises and to set us free.

And made intercession for the transgressors. There he commends His patience to us. He was heartily glad to do it. First, He depicts the suffering, second, the kind of suffering, third, the power of the suffering, and fourth, His patience. Thus, He compassionately prayed for transgressors and crucifiers, shed tears for them, and did not deal with them with threats. Who can place the Christ thus depicted in love into his heart, as He is here described? Oh, we would be blessed people if we could believe this most noble text, which must be magnified. I would wish it to be honored in the church, so that we might accustom ourselves to an alert study of this text, to bring us to see Christ as none other than the One who bears and shoulders the burden of our sins. This figure is a solace to the afflicted, but to snoring readers these are nothing but idle words.

Luther regards the Sermon on the Mount as a source of comfort for Christians and a source of irritation for the Jews. By reading it Christians understand the love of God and learn to depend on Him for comfort. He renounces the idol mammon, which is money or whatever source of comfort the nonbeliever seeks to depend on.

For Luther the Beatitudes represent the antithesis to what the world says will bring success. The secular realm depends on such temporal items as the possession of money, property, power, and the like for its feeble support. This dependence is inappropriate for the Christian, whose true happiness rests on God and what He alone provides. While it is true that the Christian has to endure hardship in this life; Luther encourages the Christian to keep his eyes on the glory of heaven.

In this sermon Luther does an exceptional job of contrasting the insubstantial, useless wares of the world with the hope that is to be found only in Christ. All that one need do is exercise patience; peace will come soon enough. To live in this life means possible hunger, thirst, oppression, and poverty. But for those who come to Christ, all these problems will be resolved.

CHAPTER FOUR

Sermon on the Mount: the Beatitudes

**Blessed are the spiritually poor, for theirs
is the kingdom of heaven.**

This is a fine, sweet, and friendly beginning for
His instruction and preaching. He does not come like
Moses or a teacher of the law, with demands, threats,
and terrors, but in a very friendly way, with enticements,
allurements, and pleasant promises. In fact, if it were
not for this report which has preserved for us all the first
dear words that the Lord Christ preached, curiosity
would drive and impel everyone to run all the way to
Jerusalem, or even to the end of the world, just to hear
one word of it. You would find plenty of money to build
such a road well! And everyone would proudly boast that
he had heard or read the very word that the Lord Christ
had preached. How wonderfully happy the man would
seem who succeeded in this! That is exactly how it

would really be if we had none of this in written form, even though there might be a great deal written by others. Everyone would say, "Yes, I heard what Saint Paul and His other apostles have taught, but I would much rather hear what He Himself spoke and preached."

But now since it is so common that everyone has it written in a book and can read it every day, no one thinks of it as anything special or precious. Yes, we grow sated and neglect it, as if it had been spoken by some shoemaker rather than the High Majesty of heaven. Therefore, it is in punishment for our ingratitude and neglect that we get so little out of it and never feel nor taste what a treasure, power, and might there is in the words of Christ. But whoever has the grace to recognize it as the Word of God rather than the word of man, will also think of it more highly and dearly, and will never grow sick and tired of it.

Friendly and sweet as this sermon is for Christians, who are His disciples, just so irksome and unbearable it is for the Jews and their great saints. From the very beginning He hits them hard with these words, rejecting and condemning their teaching, preaching the exact opposite, yes, pronouncing woe upon their life and teaching, as Luke 6:24–26 shows. The essence of their teaching was, "If a man is successful here on earth, he is blessed and well off." That was all they aimed for, that if they were pious and served God, He should give them plenty upon earth and deprive them of nothing. Thus, David says of them in Psalm 144:13–15, "This is their teaching, that all their corners and garners should be full of grain and their fields full of sheep that bear often and much, and of cattle that labor much, with no harm or failure or mischance or distress coming upon them. Happy are such people!"

In opposition to this, Christ opens His mouth here and says that something is necessary other than the possession of enough on earth, as if He were to say, "My dear disciples, when you come to preach among the people, you will find out that this is their teaching and belief: 'Whoever is rich or powerful is completely blessed; on the other hand, whoever is poor and miserable is rejected and condemned before God.'" The Jews were firmly persuaded that if a man was successful, this was a sign that he had a gracious God, and vice versa. The reason for this was the fact that they had many great promises from God regarding the temporal, physical goods that He would grant to the pious. They counted upon these, in the opinion that if they had this, they were right with Him. The book of Job is addressed to this theory. His friends argue and dispute with him about this and insist that he is being punished this way because of some great sin he must have knowingly committed against God. Therefore he ought to admit it, be converted, and become pious, that God might lift the punishment from him.

At the outset, therefore, it was necessary for [Christ's] sermon to overthrow this delusion and to tear it out of their hearts as one of the greatest obstacles to faith and a great support for the idol mammon in their heart. Such a doctrine could have no other consequence than to make people greedy, so that everyone would be interested only in amassing plenty and in having a good time, without need or trouble. And everyone would have to conclude, "If that man is blessed who succeeds and has plenty, I must see to it that I do not fall behind."

This is still what the whole world believes today, especially the Turks, who draw their reliance and strength from it, coming to the conclusion that they could not have had so much success and victory if they had not been the people of God to whom He was gracious in preference to all others. Among us, too, the whole papacy believes this. Their doctrine and life are founded only upon their having enough; therefore, they have assembled all the goods of the world, as everyone can see. In short, this is the greatest and most universal belief or religion on earth. On it all men depend according to their flesh and blood, and they cannot regard anything else as blessedness. That is why He preaches a totally new sermon here for the Christians: if they are a failure, if they have to suffer poverty and do without riches, power, honor, and good days, they will still be blessed and have not a temporal reward, but a different, eternal one; they will have enough in the kingdom of heaven.

But you say, "What? Must all Christians, then, be poor? Dare none of them have money, property, popularity, power, and the like? What are the rich to do, people like princes, lords, and kings? Must they surrender all their property and honor, or buy the kingdom of heaven from the poor, as some have taught?" Answer: No. It does not say that whoever wants to have the kingdom of heaven must buy it from the poor, but that he must be poor himself and be found among the poor. It is put clearly and candidly, "Blessed are the poor." Yet the little word "spiritually" is added, so that nothing is accomplished when someone is physically poor and has no money or goods. Having money, property, land, and retinue outwardly is not wrong in itself. It is God's gift and ordinance. No one is blessed, therefore, because he is a beggar and owns nothing of his own. The command is to be "spiritually poor." I said at the very beginning that Christ is not dealing here at all with the secular realm and order, but that He wants to discuss only the spiritual—how to live before God, above and beyond the external.

Having money, property, honor, power, land, and servants belongs to the secular realm; without these it could not endure. Therefore a lord or prince should not and cannot be poor, because for his office and station he must have all sorts of goods like these. This does not mean, therefore, that one must be poor in the sense of having nothing at all of his own. The world could not endure if we were all to be beggars and to have nothing. The head of a household could not support his household and servants if he himself had nothing at all. In short, physical poverty is not the answer. There is many a beggar getting bread at our door more arrogant and wicked than any rich man, and many a miserly, stingy peasant who is harder to get along with than any lord or prince.

So be poor or rich physically and externally, as it is granted to you—God does not ask about this—and know that before God, in his heart, everyone must be spiritually poor. That is, he must not set his confidence, comfort, and trust on temporal goods, nor hang his heart upon them and make mammon his idol. David was an outstanding king, and he really had his wallet and treasury full of money, his barns full of grain, his land full of all kinds of goods and provisions. In spite of all this he had to be a poor beggar spiritually, as he sings of himself, "I am poor, and a guest in the land, like all my fathers" (Ps. 39:12). Look at the king, sitting amid such possessions, a lord over land and people; yet he does not dare to call himself anything but a guest or a pilgrim, one who walks around on the street because he has no place to stay. This is truly a heart that does not tie itself to property and riches; but though it has [possessions,] it behaves as if it had nothing, as Saint Paul boasts of the Christians, "As poor, yet making many rich; as having nothing, and yet possessing everything" (2 Cor. 6:10).

All this is intended to say that while we live here, we should use all temporal goods and physical necessities, the way a guest does in a strange place, where he stays overnight and leaves in the morning. He needs no more than bed and board and dare not say, "This is mine, here I will stay." Nor dare he take possession of the property as though it belonged to him by right; otherwise he would soon hear the host say to him, "My friend, don't you know that you are a guest here? Go back where you belong." That is the way it is here too. The temporal goods you have, God has given to you for this life. He does permit you to use them and with them to fill the bag of worms[1] that you wear around your neck. But you should not fasten or hang your heart on them as though you were going to live forever. You should always go on and consider another, higher, and better treasure, which is your own and which will last forever.

This is said coarsely for the common man. Thus, he will learn to understand what it means in scriptural language to be "spiritually poor" or poor before God. We should not evaluate things externally, on the basis of money and property or of deficits and surpluses. For, as we have said above, we see that the poorest and most miserable beggars are the worst and most desperate rascals and dare to commit every kind of mischief and evil tricks, which fine, upstanding people, rich citizens or

---

[1] A frequent designation of the body in Luther.

lords and princes, do not do. On the other hand, many saintly people who had plenty of money and property, honor, land, and retinue, still were poor amid all this property. We should evaluate things on the basis of the heart. We must not be overly concerned whether we have something or nothing, much or little. And whatever we do have in the way of possessions, we should always treat it as though we did not have it, being ready at any time to lose it and always keeping our hearts set on the kingdom of heaven (Col. 3:2).

Then, too, a man is called "rich" in Scripture, even though he does not have any money or property, if he scrambles and scratches for them and can never get enough of them. These are the very ones whom the Gospel calls "rich bellies,"[2] who in the midst of great wealth have the very least and are never satisfied with what God grants them. That is so because the Gospel looks into the heart, which is crammed full of money and property, and evaluates on the basis of this, though there may be nothing in the wallet or the treasury. On the other hand, it also calls a man "poor" according to the condition of his heart, though he may have his treasury, house, and hearth full. Thus the Christian faith goes straight ahead. It looks at neither poverty nor riches, but only at the condition of the heart. If there is a greedy belly there, the man is called "spiritually rich"; on the other hand, he is called "spiritually poor" if he does not depend upon these things and can empty his heart of them. As Christ says elsewhere, "He who forsakes houses, land, children, or wife, will receive a hundredfold, and besides he will inherit eternal life" (Matt. 19:29). By this He seeks to rescue their hearts from regarding property as their

---

[2] It is not clear which passage of the Gospels Luther has in mind here; possibly it is Luke 12:16–21.

treasure, and to comfort His own who must forsake it; even in this life they will receive more than they leave behind.

We are not to run away from property, house, home, wife, and children, wandering around the countryside as a burden to other people. This is what the Anabaptist sect does, and they accuse us of not preaching the gospel rightly because we keep house and home and stay with wife and children. No, He does not want such crazy saints! This is what it means: in our hearts we should be able to leave house and home, wife and children. Even though we continue to live among them, eating with them and serving them out of love, as God has commanded, still we should be able, if necessary, to give them up at any time for God's sake. If you are able to do this, you have forsaken everything, in the sense that your heart is not taken captive but remains pure of greed and of dependence, trust, and confidence in anything. A rich man may properly be called "spiritually poor" without discarding his possessions. But when the necessity arises, then let him do so in God's name, not because he would like to get away from wife and children, house and home, but because, as long as God wills it, he would rather keep them and serve Him thereby, yet is also willing to let Him take them back.

So you see what it means to be "poor" spiritually and before God, to have nothing spiritually and to forsake everything. Now look at the promise which Christ appends when He says, "For of such is the kingdom of heaven." This is certainly a great, wonderful, and glorious promise. Because we are willing to be poor here and pay no attention to temporal goods, we are to have a beautiful, glorious, great, and eternal possession in heaven. And because you have given up a crumb, which you still may use as long and as much as you can have it, you are to receive a crown, to be a citizen and a lord in heaven. This would stir us if we really wanted to be Christians and if we believed that His words are true. But no one cares who is saying this, much less what He is saying. They let it go in one ear and out the other, so that no one troubles himself about it or takes it to heart.

With these words [Christ] shows that no one can understand this unless he is already a real Christian. This point and all the rest that follow are purely fruits of faith, which the Holy Spirit Himself must create in the heart. Where there is no faith, there the kingdom of heaven also will remain outside; nor will spiritual poverty, meekness, and the like follow, but there will remain only scratching and scraping, quarrels and riots over temporal goods. Therefore, it is all over for such worldly hearts, so that they never learn or experience what spiritual poverty is, and neither believe nor care what He says and promises about the kingdom of heaven.

Yet for their sakes He so arranges and orders things that whoever is not willing to be spiritually poor in God's name and for the sake of the kingdom of heaven, must still be poor in the devil's name and not have any thanks for it. God has so hung the greedy to their bellies that they are never satisfied or happy with their greedily gained goods. Sir Greed is such a jolly guest that he does not let anyone rest. He seeks, pushes, and hunts without stopping, so that he cannot enjoy his precious property for a single hour. Thus Solomon the preacher wonders and says, "Is it not a sore affliction that God gives a man wealth and possessions, land and retinue, and yet he is not capable of enjoying them?" (Eccles. 6:2). He must always be afraid, troubled, and concerned about how he is going to keep it and expand it, lest it disappear or diminish. He is so completely its prisoner that he cannot enjoy spending a [coin] of it. But if there were a heart that could be content and satisfied, it would have rest and the kingdom of heaven besides. Otherwise, amid great possessions and with its greed, it must have purgatory here and hell-fire hereafter. As they say, "Here you travel in a wheelbarrow, but there on one wheel,"[3] that is, you have trouble and anxiety here, but bitter grief hereafter.

This is the way God always works, so that His Word remains true and no one is saved or satisfied except the Christian. Though the others have everything, their lot is never any better; indeed, it is never as good, and they must still remain poor beggars as far as their heart is concerned. The difference is that the former are glad to be poor and depend upon an imperishable, eternal possession, that is, upon the kingdom of heaven, and are the blessed children of God; but the latter are greedy for temporal goods, and yet they get what they want, but must eternally be the victims of the devil's tortures besides. In short, there is no difference between a beggar before the door and such a miserable belly, except that the one has nothing and lets himself be put off with a crust of bread, while the other, the more he has, the less satisfied he is, even though he were to get all the goods and money in the world in one pile.

As I have said, therefore, this sermon does the world no good and accomplishes nothing for it. The world stubbornly insists upon being right. It refuses to believe a thing, but must have it before its very eyes and hold it in

---

[3]The reference is to a German proverb.

its hand, saying, "A bird in the hand is worth two in the bush."[4] Therefore, Christ also lets them go. He does not want to force anyone or drag him in by the hair. But He gives His faithful advice to all who will let Him advise them, and He holds before us the dearest promises. If you want it, you have peace and quiet in your heart here, and hereafter whatever your heart desires forever. If you do not want it, have your own way, and rather have sorrow and misfortune both here and hereafter. For we see and experience that everything depends upon being content and not clinging to temporal goods. There are many people whose hearts God can fill so that they may have only a morsel of bread and yet are cheerful and more content than any prince or king. In brief, such a person is a rich lord and emperor, and he need have no worry, trouble, or sorrow. This is the first point of this sermon: whoever wants to have enough here and hereafter, let him see to it that he is not greedy or grasping. Let him accept and use what God gives him, and live by his labor in faith. Then he will have paradise and even the kingdom of heaven here, as Saint Paul also says, "Godliness is of value in every way, as it holds promise for the present life and also for the life to come" (1 Tim. 4:8).

Blessed are those who mourn, for they shall be comforted.

He began this sermon against the doctrine and belief of the Jews—in fact, not only of the Jews but of the whole world which, even at its best, sticks to the delusion that it is well off if it just has property, popularity,

---

[4]The original phrasing of the proverb which Luther cites is "It is better to hold a sparrow in your hand than to stare at a crane in the air."

and its mammon here, and which serves God only for this purpose. In the same way He now continues, overturning even what they thought was the best and most blessed life on earth, one in which a person would attain to good and quiet days and would not have to endure discomfort, as Psalm 73:5 describes it: "They are not in trouble as other men are; they are not stricken like other men."

For that is the highest thing that men want, to have joy and happiness and to be without trouble. Now Christ turns the page and says exactly the opposite; He calls "blessed" those who sorrow and mourn. Thus throughout, all these statements are aimed and directed against the world's way of thinking, the way it would like to have things. It does not want to endure hunger, trouble, dishonor, unpopularity, injustice, and violence; and it calls "blessed" those who can avoid all these things.

So He wants to say here that there must be another life than the life of their quests and thoughts, and that a Christian must count on sorrow and mourning in the world. Whoever does not want to do this may have a good time here and live to his heart's desire, but hereafter he will have to mourn forever. As He says, "Woe unto you that laugh and have a good time now! For you shall have to mourn and weep" (Luke 6:25). This is how it went with the rich man in Luke 16. He lived luxuriously and joyfully all his life, decked out in expensive silk and purple. He thought he was a great saint and well off in the sight of God because He had given him so much property. Meanwhile, he let poor Lazarus lie before his door daily, full of sores, in hunger and trouble and great misery. But what kind of judgment did he finally hear when he was lying in hell? "Remember that in your lifetime you received good things, but Lazarus, evil things. Therefore you are now in anguish, but he is comforted" (Luke 16:25).

See, this is the same text as "Blessed are those who mourn, for they shall be comforted," which is as much as saying, "Those who seek [to] have nothing but joy and fun here shall weep and howl forever."

You may ask again, "What are we to do, then? Is everyone to be damned who laughs, sings, dances, dresses well, eats, and drinks? After all, we read about kings and saints who were cheerful and lived well. Paul is an especially wonderful saint; he wants us to be cheerful all the time (Phil. 4:4), and he says, 'Rejoice with those who rejoice,' and again, 'Weep with those who weep' (Rom. 12:15). That sounds contradictory, to be joyful all the time and yet to weep and mourn with others."

Answer: I said before that having riches is not sinful, nor is it forbidden. So also being joyful, eating and drinking well, is not sinful or damnable; nor is having honor and a good name. Still I am supposed to be "blessed" if I do not have these things or can do without them, and instead suffer poverty, misery, shame, and persecution. So both of these things are here and must be—being sad and being happy, eating and going hungry, as Paul boasts about himself, "I have learned the art, wherever I am, to be content. I know how to be abased, and I know how to abound; in any and all circumstances I have learned the secret of facing plenty and hunger, abundance and want" (Phil. 4:11, 12). And in 2 Corinthians 6:8–10: "In honor and dishonor, in ill repute and good repute; as dying, and, behold, we live; as sorrowful, yet always rejoicing."

So this is what it means: a man is called "spiritually poor," not because he has no money or anything of his own, but because he does not covet it or set his comfort and trust upon it as though it were his kingdom of heaven. So also a man is said to "mourn and be sorrowful"—not if his head is always drooping and his face is always sour and never smiling; but if he does not depend upon having a good time and living it up, the way the world does, which yearns for nothing but having sheer joy and fun here, revels in it, and neither thinks nor cares about the state of God or men.

In this way many great and outstanding people, kings and others, who were Christians, have had to mourn and be sorrowful, though in the eyes of the world they lived a glorious life. Thus, throughout the Psalter David complains about his weeping and sorrow. Now, too, I could easily cite examples of great men, lords and princes, who have experienced and learned this about the gracious Gospel, at the recent Diet of Augsburg and elsewhere. Externally they lived well, dressed in princely fashion in silk and gold, and looked like people for whom life was a bed of roses.[5] But daily they had to be right in the midst of poisonous snakes; and in their heart they had to experience such unheard of arrogance, insolence, and shame, so many evil tricks and words from the vile papists, who delighted in embittering their hearts and, as far as possible, in denying them a single happy hour. Thus, they had to stew within themselves and do nothing but lament before God with sighs and tears. Such people know something of what the statement means: "Blessed are those who mourn and are sorrowful," though they do not always show it. They eat and drink with other people and sometimes laugh and joke with them, to forget their sorrow. You must not suppose that "to mourn" means only

---

[5]The original expression is "People who were traveling on sheer roses."

to weep and cry and scream, like women and children. It is not the real and most profound mourning when it has come over the heart and breaks forth through the eyes, but when really great shocks come, which strike and shake the heart so that one cannot cry and dare not complain to anyone.

Therefore, mourning and sorrow are not a rare plant among Christians, in spite of outward appearances. They would like to be joyful in Christ, outwardly, too, as much as they can. Daily, whenever they look at the world, they must see and feel in their heart so much wickedness, arrogance, contempt, and blasphemy of God and His Word, so much sorrow and sadness, which the devil causes in both the spiritual and the secular realm. Therefore, they cannot have many joyful thoughts, and their spiritual joy is very weak. If they were to look at this continually and did not turn their eyes away from time to time, they could not be happy for a moment. It is bad enough that this really happens oftener than they would like, so that they do not have to go out looking for it.

Therefore, simply begin to be a Christian, and you will soon find out what it means to mourn and be sorrowful. If you can do nothing else, then get married, settle down, and make a living in faith. Love the Word of God, and do what is required of you in your station. Then you will experience, both from your neighbors and in your own household, that things will not go as you might wish. You will be hindered and hemmed in on every side, so that you will suffer enough and see enough to make your heart sad. But especially the dear preachers must learn this well and be disciplined daily with all sorts of envy, hatred, scorn, ridicule, ingratitude, contempt, and blasphemy. In addition, they have to stew inside, so that their hearts and souls are pierced through and continually tormented.

Because the world does not want to have such mourning and sorrow, it seeks out those stations and ways of life where it can have fun and does not have to suffer anything from anyone, as the monks' and priests' station used to be. It cannot stand the idea that in a divine station it should serve other people with nothing but care, toil, and trouble, and get nothing as a reward for this but ingratitude, contempt and other malicious treatment. Therefore, when things do not go with it as it wishes and one person looks at another with a sour face, all they can do is to batter things with cursing and swearing, and with their fists too, and be ready to put up property and reputation, land and servants. But God arranges things so that they still cannot get off too easily, without seeing or suffering any trouble at all. What He gives them as a reward for not wanting to suffer is this: they still have to suffer, but by their anger and impatience they make it twice as great and difficult, and without finding any comfort or a good conscience. The Christians have the advantage that though they mourn too, they shall be comforted and be blessed both here and hereafter.

Therefore, whoever wants to have fellowship with Christians and does not want to be an outright child of the world, let him be on the list of those who are willing to sigh and mourn, so that he may be comforted, as this promise says. We have an instance of this in Ezekiel 9. God sent out six men with "destroying weapons" against the city of Jerusalem, but one of them He sent with a writing case; he was to go through the middle of the city and put a mark upon the foreheads of those who sighed and groaned over the shameful situation and who had to watch it with sorrow in their hearts. Whoever was marked this way was to live, but all the others were to be killed. You see, this is the Christians' advantage. In the world they have to see nothing but sorrow and trouble. Yet when the world is at its smuggest and is riding along on sheer joy, suddenly the wheel turns, and a misfortune comes upon them in which they have to stay and perish. But the Christians are rescued and saved, the way Lot was saved in Sodom; for as Saint Peter says, they had long vexed and distressed his heart with their licentiousness (2 Pet. 2:7, 8). Let the world, therefore, laugh now and live riotously in its delights and pleasures. Though you have to mourn and be sorrowful and daily see your heart troubled, take it in stride and hold fast to this saying. Let it satisfy and comfort you. Outwardly, too, refresh yourself and be as cheerful as possible.

Those who mourn this way are entitled to have fun and to take it wherever they can so that they do not completely collapse for sorrow. Christ also adds these words and promises this consolation so that they do not despair in their sorrow nor let the joy of their heart be taken away and extinguished altogether, but mix this mourning with comfort and refreshment. Otherwise, if they never had any comfort or joy, they would have to languish and wither away. No man can stand continual mourning. It sucks out the very strength and savor of the body, as the wise man says, "Sadness has killed many people" (Ecclesiasticus 30:25); and again, "A downcast spirit dries up the marrow in the bones" (Prov. 17:22). Therefore, we should not neglect this but should command and urge such people to have a good time once in a while if possible, or at least to temper their sorrow and forget it for a while.

Thus Christ does not want to urge continual mourning

and sorrow. He wants to warn against those who seek to escape all mourning and to have nothing but fun and all their comfort here. And He wants to teach His Christians, when things go badly for them and they have to mourn, to know that it is God's good pleasure and to make it theirs as well, not to curse or rage or despair as though their God did not want to be gracious. When this happens, the bitter draft should be mixed and made milder with honey and sugar. He promises here that this is pleasing to Him; and He calls them "blessed," comforting them here, and hereafter taking the sorrow away from them completely. Therefore, say good-by to the world and to all those who harm us, in the name of their lord, the devil. And let us sing this song and be joyful in the name of God and Christ. Their outcome will surely not be the one they want. Now they take pleasure in our misfortune and do much to harm us. Still we take heart, and we shall live to see that at the last they will have to howl and weep when we are comforted and happy.

Blessed are the meek, for they shall inherit the earth.

This statement fits the first one well, when He said, "Blessed are the spiritually poor." For as He promises the kingdom of heaven and an eternal possession there, so here He also adds a promise about this temporal life and about possessions here on earth. But how does being poor harmonize with inheriting the land? It might seem that the preacher has forgotten how He began. Whoever is to inherit land and possessions cannot be poor. By "inheriting the land" here and having all sorts of possessions here on earth, He does not mean that everyone is to inherit a whole country; otherwise God would have to create more worlds. But God confers possessions upon everyone in such a way that He gives a man wife, children, cattle, house, and home, and whatever pertains to these, so that he can stay on the land where he lives and have dominion over his possessions. This is the way Scripture customarily speaks, as Psalm 37 says several times, "Those who wait for the Lord will inherit the land"; and again, "His blessed ones inherit the land." Therefore, He adds His own gloss here: to be "spiritually poor," as He used the expression before, does not mean to be a beggar or to discard money and possessions. For here He tells them to live and remain in the land and to manage earthly possessions, as we shall hear later.

What does it mean, then, to be meek? From the outset you must realize that Christ is not speaking at all about the government and its work, whose property it is not to be meek, as we use the word in German, but to bear the sword (Rom. 13:4) for the punishment of those who do wrong (1 Pet. 2:14), and to wreak a vengeance and a wrath that are called the vengeance and wrath of God. He is only talking about how individuals are to live in relation to others, apart from official position and authority—how father and mother are to live, not in relation to their children nor in their official capacity as father and mother, but in relation to those for whom they are not father and mother, like neighbors and other people. I have often said that we must sharply distinguish between these two, the office and the person. The man who is called Hans or Martin is a man quite different from the one who is called elector or doctor or preacher. Here we have two different persons in one man. The one is that in which we are created and born, according to which we are alike—man or woman or child, young or old. But once you are born, God adorns and dresses you up as another person. He makes you a child and me a father, one a master and another a servant, one a prince and another a citizen. Then this one is called a divine person, one who holds a divine office and goes about clothed in its dignity—not simply Hans or Nick, but the Prince of Saxony, father, or master. He is not talking about this person here, letting it alone in its own office and rule, as He has ordained it. He is talking merely about how each individual, natural person is to behave in relation to others.

Therefore, if we have an office or a governmental position, we must be sharp and strict, we must get angry and punish; for here we must do what God puts into our hand and commands us to do for His sake. In other relations, in what is unofficial, let everyone learn for himself to be meek toward everyone else, that is, not to deal with his neighbor unreasonably, hatefully, or vengefully, like the people whom they call "Headlong Hans." They refuse to put up with anything or to yield an inch, but they tear up the world and the hills and want to uproot the trees. They never listen to anyone nor excuse him for anything. They immediately buckle on their armor, thinking of nothing but how to take vengeance and hit back. This does not forbid the government to punish and to wreak vengeance in the name of God. But neither does it grant license to a wicked judge, burgomaster, lord, or prince to confuse these two persons and to reach beyond his official authority through personal malice or envy or hate or hostility, as commonly happens, under the cloak and cover of his office and legal right. This would be as though, in the name of the government, our neighbors wanted to take some action against us which they could not get away with otherwise.

He is talking here especially to His Jews, as He had begun. They always insisted that they were not supposed to suffer anything from a Gentile or stranger and that they had a right to avenge themselves immediately. For this purpose they cited sayings from Moses, such as Deuteronomy 28:13: "The Lord will make you the head, and not the tail; and you shall tend upward only, and not downward." There would be nothing wrong with this. But it means that if God Himself does this, then it is well done. It is one thing if He commands it and says, "I will do it," and quite another thing if we do it ourselves, without authorization. What He says should and must happen; what we say happens if it can, or maybe it does not happen at all. So you have no right to lay claim to this promise for yourself and to count on it when you want to do something which He ought to do, and you refuse to wait until He commands you to do it.

You see, then, that here Christ is rebuking those crazy saints who think that everyone is master of the whole world and is entitled to be delivered from all suffering, to roar and bluster and violently to defend his property. And He teaches us that whoever wants to rule and possess his property, his possessions, house, and home in peace, must be meek, so that he may overlook things and act reasonably, putting up with just as much as he possibly can. It is inevitable that your neighbor will sometimes do you injury or harm, either accidentally or maliciously. If he did it accidentally, you do not improve the situation by refusing or being unable to endure anything. If he did it maliciously, you only irritate him by your violent scratching and pounding; meanwhile he is laughing at you and enjoying the fact that he is baiting and troubling you, so that you still cannot have any peace or quietly enjoy what is yours.

So select one of the two, whichever you prefer: either to live in human society with meekness and patience and to hold on to what you have with peace and a good conscience; or boisterously and blusterously to lose what is yours, and to have no peace besides. There stands the decree, "The meek shall inherit the earth." Just take a look for yourself at the queer characters who are always arguing and squabbling about property and other things. They refuse to give in to anybody, but insist on rushing everything through headlong, regardless of whether their quarreling and squabbling costs them more than they could ever gain. Ultimately they lose their land and servants, house and home, and get unrest and a bad conscience thrown in. And God adds His blessing to it, saying, "Do not be meek, then, so that you may not keep your precious land, nor enjoy your morsel in peace."

But if you want to do right and have rest, let your neighbor's malice and viciousness smother and burn itself out. Otherwise you can do nothing more pleasing to the devil or more harmful to yourself than to lose your temper and make a racket. Do you have a government? Then register a complaint, and let it see to it. The government has the charge not to permit the harsh oppression of the innocent. God will also overrule so that His Word and ordinance may abide and you may inherit the land according to this promise. Thus you will have rest and God's blessing, but your neighbor will have unrest together with God's displeasure and curse. This sermon is intended only for those who are Christians, who believe and know that they have their treasure in heaven, where it is secure for them and cannot be taken away. Hence, they must have enough here, too, even though they do not have treasuries and pockets full of [money]. Since you know this, why let your joy be disturbed and taken away? Why cause yourself disquiet and rob yourself of this magnificent promise?

See now that you have three points with three rich promises. Whoever is a Christian must have enough of both the temporal and the eternal, though here he must suffer much both outwardly and inwardly, in the heart. On the other hand, because the worldlings refuse to endure poverty or trouble or violence, they neither have the kingdom of heaven nor enjoy temporal goods peacefully and quietly. You can read more about this in Psalm 37, which is the right gloss on this passage, richly describing how the meek are to inherit the land while the ungodly are to be exterminated.

Blessed are those who hunger and thirst for righteousness, for they shall be satisfied.

"Righteousness" in this passage must not be taken in the sense of that principal Christian righteousness by which a person becomes pious and acceptable to God. I have said before that these eight items are nothing but instruction about the fruits and good works of a Christian. Before these must come faith, as the tree and chief part or summary of a man's righteousness and blessedness, without any work or merit of his; out of which faith these items all must grow and follow. Therefore, take this in the sense of the outward righteousness before the world, which we maintain in our relations with each other. Thus, the short and simple meaning of these words is this: that man is righteous and blessed who continually works and strives with all his might to promote the general welfare and the proper behavior of everyone and who helps to maintain and support this by word and deed, by precept and example.

Now, this is also a precious point, embracing very many good works, but by no means a common thing. Let me illustrate with an example. If a preacher wants to qualify under this point, he must be ready to instruct and help everyone to perform his assigned task properly and to do what it requires. And when he sees that something is missing and things are not going right, he should be on hand to warn, rebuke, and correct by whatever method or means he can. Thus, as a preacher I dare not neglect my office. Nor dare the others neglect theirs, which is to follow my teaching and preaching. In this way the right thing is done on both sides. Now, where there are people who earnestly take it upon themselves to do right gladly and to be found engaged in the right works and ways, such people "hunger and thirst for righteousness." If this were the situation, there would be no rascality or injustice, but sheer righteousness and blessedness on earth. What is the righteousness of the world except that in his station everyone should do his duty? That means that the rights of every station should be respected—those of the man, the woman, the child, the manservant, and the maid in the household, the citizen of the city in the land. And it is all contained in this, that those who are charged with overseeing and ruling other people should execute this office diligently, carefully, and faithfully, and that the others should also render their due service and obedience to them faithfully and willingly.

It is not by accident that he uses the term "hunger and thirst for righteousness." By it He intends to point out that this requires great earnestness, longing, eagerness, and unceasing diligence and that where this hunger and thirst [are] lacking, everything will fail. The reason is that there are too many great hindrances. They come from the devil, who is blocking and barricading the way everywhere. They also come from the world—that is, his children—which is so wicked that it cannot stand a pious man who wants to do right himself or to help other people do so, but plagues him in every way, [so] that he finally becomes tired and perplexed over the whole business. It is painful to see how shamefully people behave, and to get no reward for pure kindness except ingratitude, contempt, hate, and persecution. For this reason, many people who could not stand the sight of such evil conduct finally despaired over it, ran away from human society into the desert, and became monks, so that the saying has repeatedly been verified: "Despair makes a man a monk."[6] A person may not trust himself to make his own living and run into the monastery for his belly's sake, as the great crowd has done; otherwise a person may despair of the world and not trust himself in it, either to remain pious or to help people.

But this is not hungering and thirsting for righteousness. Anyone who tries to preach or rule in such a way that he lets himself become tired and impatient and be chased into a corner will not be of much help to other people. The command to you is not to crawl into a corner or into the desert, but to run out, if that is where you have been, and to offer your hands and your feet and your whole body, and to wager everything you have and can do. You should be the kind of man who is firm in the face of firmness, who will not let himself be frightened

---

[6]Part of a medieval proverb: "Despair makes a man three things—a monk, a physician, or a soldier."

off or dumbfounded or overcome by the world's ingratitude or malice, who will always hold on and push with all the might he can summon. In short, the ministry requires a hunger and thirst for righteousness that can never be curbed or stopped or sated, one that looks for nothing and cares for nothing except the accomplishment and maintenance of the right, despising everything that hinders this end. If you cannot make the world completely pious, then do what you can. It is enough that you have done your duty and have helped a few, even if there be only one or two. If others will not follow, then in God's name let them go. You must not run away on account of the wicked, but rather conclude, "I did not undertake this for their sakes, and I shall not drop it for their sakes. Eventually some of them might come around; at least there might be fewer of them, and they may improve a little."

Here you have a comforting and certain promise, with which Christ allures and attracts His Christians: "Those who hunger and thirst for righteousness shall be filled." That is, they will be recompensed for their hunger and thirst by seeing that their work was not in vain and that at last a little flock has been brought around who have been helped. Although things are not going now as they would like and they have almost despaired over it, all this will become manifest, not only here on earth, but even more in the life hereafter, when everyone will see what sort of fruit such people have brought by their diligence and perseverance. For example, a pious preacher has snatched many souls out of the jaws of the devil and brought them to heaven; or a pious, faithful ruler has helped many lands and people, who testify that he has done so and who praise him before the whole world.

The counterfeit saints are exactly the opposite. Because of their great sanctity they forsake the world and run into the desert, or they sneak away into a corner somewhere to escape the trouble and worry that they would otherwise have to bear. They do not want to pay attention to what is going on in the world. Never once do they think of the fact that they should help or advise other people with teaching, instruction, warning, reproof, correction, or at least with prayers and sighs to God. Yes, it even disgusts and grieves them when other people become pious; for they want to be thought of as the only ones who are holy so that anyone who wants to get to heaven has to buy their good works and merits from them. In brief, they are so full of self-righteousness that they look down their noses at other poor sinners. Just so in Luke 18:11 the great pharisee in his intoxication looks down at the poor publican and spits on him. He is so much in love with himself that he pays court to God and thanks Him that he alone is pious and other people are bad.

Note that these are the people against whom Christ is speaking here, the shameful, proud, and self-sufficient spirits, who are tickled, pleased, and overjoyed over the fact that other people are not pious, whereas they ought to pity them, sympathize with them, and help them. All they can do is to despise, slander, judge, and condemn everyone else; everything must be stench and filth except what they themselves do. But going out to admonish and help a poor, frail sinner—this they avoid as they would avoid the devil. Hence they will have to hear again what Christ cries out against them in Luke 6:25, "Woe to you that are full, for you shall hunger." As those who now hunger and thirst shall be filled, so these others must hunger forever; though they are full and sated now, no one has ever got any benefit from them or been able to praise them for ever helping anyone or setting him aright. There you have a summary of the meaning of this passage, which, as I have said, embraces many good works, indeed, all the good works by which a man may live right by himself in human society and help to give success to all sorts of offices and stations.

Blessed are the merciful, for they shall obtain mercy.

This is also an outstanding fruit of faith, and it follows well upon what went before. Anyone who is supposed to help other people and to contribute to the common weal and success should also be kind and merciful. He should not immediately raise a rumpus and start a riot if something is missing or if things do not go as they should, as long as there is still some hope for improvement. One of the virtues of counterfeit sanctity is that it cannot have pity or mercy for the frail and weak, but insists on the strictest enforcement and the purest selection; as soon as there is even a minor flaw, all mercy is gone, and there is nothing but fuming and fury. Saint Gregory also teaches us how to recognize this when he says, "True justice shows mercy, but false justice shows indignation." True holiness is merciful and sympathetic, but all that false holiness can do is to rage and fume. Yet it does so, as they boast, "out of zeal for justice"; that is, it is done through love and zeal for righteousness.

The whole world is being forced to the conclusion that they have been carrying on their mischief and violence under the lovely and excellent pretext and cover of doing it for the sake of righteousness. In the same way, both in the past and in the present, they have been exercising their enmity and treachery against the Gospel under the guise of defending the truth and exterminating heresy. For this they want God to crown them and to elevate them to heaven, as a reward for those who out of great thirst and hunger for righteousness persecute, strangle, and burn His saints.

They want to make the claim and to give the impression, even more than the true saints, that they hunger and thirst for righteousness. They put up such a good front and use such beautiful words that they think even God Himself will not know any better. But the noble tree is known by its fruits. When they should demand justice, that is, the proper administration of both the spiritual and the temporal realm, they do not do so. It never enters their mind to instruct and improve anyone. They themselves live in continual vice; and if anyone denounces their behavior or does not praise it and do as they want, he must be a heretic and let himself be damned. You see, that is how it is with every counterfeit saint. His self-made holiness makes him so proud that he despises everyone else and cannot have a kind and merciful heart.

Therefore, this is a necessary warning against such abominable saints. If a man deals with his neighbor in an effort to help and correct him in his station and way of life, he should still take care to be merciful and to forgive. In this way people will see that your aim really is righteousness and not the gratification of your own malice and anger; for you are righteous enough to deal in a friendly and gentle manner with the man who is willing to forsake his unrighteousness and improve himself, and you tolerate and endure his fault or weakness until he comes around. But if you try all this and find no hope for improvement, then you may give him up and turn him over to those whose duty it is to punish.

Now, this is the one aspect of mercy, that one gladly

forgives the sinful and the frail. The other is to do good also to those who are outwardly poor or in need of help; on the basis of Matthew 25:35 we call these "works of mercy." The arrogant Jewish saints knew nothing about this aspect either. There was nothing in them but ice and frost—yes, a heart as hard as a block of stone—and not a single loving drop of blood that took pleasure in doing good for a neighbor, nor any mercy that forgave sin. All they were concerned about and thought about was their own belly, even though another man might have been starving to death. Thus, there is much more mercy among public sinners than there is in such a saint. This is how it has to be; for they praise only themselves and regard only themselves as holy, despising everyone else as worthless. They suppose that the whole world must serve them and give them plenty, while they are under no obligation to render anyone any service.

Hence, this sermon and exhortation seems contemptible and useless to such saints. The only pupils it finds are those who already cling to Christ and believe in Him. They know of no holiness of their own. On the basis of the preceding items they are poor, miserable, meek, really hungry and thirsty; they are inclined not to despise anyone, but to assume and to sympathize with the need of everyone else. To them applies the comforting promise, "It is well with you who are merciful. For you will find pure mercy in turn, both here and hereafter, and a mercy which inexpressibly surpasses all human kindness and mercy." There is no comparison between our mercy and God's, nor between our possessions and the eternal possessions in the kingdom of heaven. So pleased is He with our kindness to our neighbor that for one [small coin] He promises us a hundred thousand [pieces of gold] if we have need of them, and for a drink of water, the kingdom of heaven (Matt. 10:42).

Now, if anyone will not let himself be moved by this wonderful and comforting promise, let him turn the page and hear another judgment: "Woe and curses upon the unmerciful, for no mercy shall be shown to them." At the present time the world is full of people, among the nobles and city people and peasants, who sin very grievously against the dear Gospel. Not only do they refuse to give support or help to poor ministers and preachers, but besides they commit theft and torment against it wherever they can, and act as if they meant to starve it out and chase it out of the world. Meanwhile they go along quite smugly, supposing that God must keep quiet about it and approve of everything they do. But it will hit them someday. I am afraid that someone will come along who will make a prophet out of me—for I have given ample warning—and treat them mercilessly, taking away their reputation and their property, their body and their life, so that the Word of God might remain true and so that he who refuses to show or to have mercy might experience endless wrath and eternal displeasure. As Saint James also says, "Judgment without mercy will be spoken over the one who has shown no mercy" (Jas. 2:13). At the Last Day, therefore, Christ will also cite this lack of mercy as the worst injury done to Him, whatever we have done out of a lack of mercy. He Himself will utter the curse, "I was hungry and thirsty, and you gave Me no food, you gave Me no drink. Depart from Me, therefore, you cursed, into eternal hell-fire" (Matt. 25:41, 42). He warns and exhorts us faithfully, out of sheer grace and mercy. Whoever does not want to accept this, let him choose the curse and eternal damnation. Think of the rich man in Luke 16; daily he saw poor Lazarus lying before his door full of sores, yet he did not have enough mercy to give him a bundle of straw or to grant him the crumbs under his table. But look how terribly he was requited; in hell he would gladly have given a hundred thousand guldens [pieces of gold] for the privilege of boasting that he had given him a thread.

Blessed are those of a pure heart, for they shall see God.

This item is rather obscure, and not very intelligible to us who have such coarse, carnal hearts and minds. It is also hidden from all the sophists, who have the reputation of being most learned, none of them can say what it means to have a "pure heart," much less what it means to "see God." With mere dreams and random thoughts they walk around things of which they have no experience. Therefore, we must look at these words according to the Scriptures and learn to understand them correctly.

They have imagined that having a pure heart means for a man to run away from human society into a corner, a monastery, or a desert, neither thinking about the world nor concerning himself with worldly affairs and business, but amusing himself only with heavenly thoughts. By this delusive doctrine they have not only beguiled and dangerously deceived themselves and other people, but have even committed the murderous crime of calling "profane" the act and stations which the world requires and which, as a matter of fact, God Himself has ordained. But Scripture speaks of this pure heart and mind in a manner that is completely consistent with being a husband, loving wife and children, thinking about them and caring for them, and paying attention to other matters involved in such a relationship. For God has commanded all of this. Whatever God has commanded cannot be profane (Acts 10:15); indeed it must be the very purity with which we see God. For example, when a judge performs his official duty in sentencing a criminal to death, that is not *his* office and work but God's. If he is a Christian, therefore, this is a good, pure, and holy work, one he could not do if he did not already have a pure heart. In the same way it must be regarded as a pure work and pure heart when a servant in the household does a dirty and repulsive job, like hauling manure or washing and cleaning children. Hence, it is a shameful perversion to disparage the relationships covered by the Ten Commandments this way and to gape at other special and showy works. As though God did not have as pure a mouth or eyes as we, or as pure a heart and hand when He creates both man and woman! Then how can such works and thoughts make a heart impure? This is the blindness and foolishness that comes upon men who despise the Word of God and who determine purity only by the outward mask and the show of works. Meanwhile, they are causing trouble with their own wandering thoughts . . . as though they wanted to climb up to heaven and grope for God, until they break their own necks in the process.

Let us understand correctly, then, what Christ calls a "pure heart." Note again that the target and object of this sermon were principally the Jews. They did not want to suffer, but sought a life of ease, pleasure, and joy; they did not want to hunger nor to be merciful, but to be smug in their exclusive piety while they judged and despised other people. In the same way, their holiness also consisted in outward cleanliness of body, skin, hair, clothes, and food, so that they did not dare to have even a speck on their clothing; if anyone touched a dead body, or had a scab or a rash on his body, he did not dare to approach other people. This is what they called "purity." "But that does not do it," says Christ, "the ones I praise are those who take pains to have a pure heart." So He says in Matthew 23:25, "You cleanse the outside of the cup and of the plate, but inside you are full of extortion and rapacity." Again, "You are like whitewashed tombs, which outwardly appear beautiful, but within they are full of dead men's bones and all uncleanness" (Matt. 23:27). This is the way it is with our clergy today. Outwardly they lead a decent life, and in the churches everything is conducted with such excellent taste and formality that it is beautiful to behold. But He does not ask for such purity. He wants to have the heart pure, though outwardly the person may be a drudge in the kitchen, black, sooty, and grimy, doing all sorts of dirty work.

Then what is a pure heart? In what does it consist? The answer can be given quickly, and you do not have to climb up to heaven or run to a monastery for it, establishing it with your own ideas. You should be on your guard against any ideas that you call your own, as if they were just so much mud and filth. And you should realize that when a monk in the monastery is sitting in deepest contemplation, excluding the world from his heart altogether, and thinking about the Lord God the way he himself paints and imagines Him, he is actually sitting—if you will pardon the expression—in the dung, not up to his knees but up to his ears. For he is proceeding on his own ideas without the Word of God; and that is sheer deception and delusion, as Scripture testifies everywhere.

What is meant by a "pure heart" is this: one that is watching and pondering what God says and replacing its own ideas with the Word of God. This alone is pure before God, yes, purity itself, which purifies everything that it includes and touches. Therefore, though a common laborer, a shoemaker, or a blacksmith may be dirty and sooty or may smell because he is covered with dirt and pitch, still he may sit at home and think, "My God has made me a man. He has given me my house, wife, and child and has commanded me to love them and to support them with my work." Note that he is pondering the Word of God in his heart; and though he stinks outwardly, inwardly he is pure incense before God. But if he attains the highest purity so that he also takes hold of the gospel and believes in Christ—without this, that purity is impossible—then he is pure completely, inwardly in his heart toward God and outwardly toward everything under him on earth. Then everything he is and does, his walking, standing, eating, and drinking, is pure for him; and nothing can make him impure. So it is when he looks at his own wife or fondles her, as the patriarch Isaac did (Gen. 26:8), which a monk regards as disgusting and defiling. For here he has the Word of God, and he knows that God has given her to him. But if he were to desert his wife and take up another, or neglect his job or duty to harm or bother other people, he would no longer be pure; for that would be contrary to God's commandment.

But so long as he sticks to these two—namely, the Word of faith toward God, which purifies the heart, and the Word of understanding, which teaches him what he is to do toward his neighbor in his station—everything is pure for him, even if with his hands and the rest of his body he handles nothing but dirt. If a poor housemaid does her duty and is a Christian in addition, then before God in heaven she is a lovely and pure beauty, one that all the angels admire and love to look at. On the other hand, if the most austere Carthusian fasts and whips himself to death, if he does nothing but weep out of sheer devotion, if he never gives the world a thought, and yet lacks faith in Christ and love for his neighbor, he is nothing but a stench and a pollution, inwardly and outwardly, so that both God and the angels find him abhorrent and disgusting.

So you see that everything depends on the Word of God. Whatever is included in that and goes in accordance with it, must be called clean, pure, and white as snow before both God and man. Therefore, Paul says, "To the pure all things are pure"; and again, "To the corrupt and unbelieving nothing is pure" (Titus 1:15). Why is this so? Because both their minds and their consciences are impure. How does this happen? Because "they profess to know God, but with their deeds they deny it" (Titus 1:16). These are the people who are abominable in the sight of God. Look how horribly the apostle paints and denounces these great Jewish saints. Take, for example, a Carthusian monk. He thinks that if he lives according to his strict rule of obedience, poverty, and celibacy, if he is isolated from the world, he is pure in every way. What is this but his own way of thinking, growing up in his own heart without the Word of God and faith? In this way monks think that they alone are pure and that other people are impure. Saint Paul calls this an "impure mind," that is, everything they think and imagine. Since this delusion and idea is impure, everything they do on the basis of it must also be impure for them. As their mind is, so is their conscience too. Though they should and could be of help to other people, they have a conscience that functions on the basis of their ideas and is bound to their cowls, cloisters, and rules. They think that if they neglected this routine even for a moment to serve their neighbor and had relations with other people, they would be committing a most grievous sin and defiling themselves altogether. The cause of all this is that they do not acknowledge God's Word and creatures, although, as Saint Paul says, "With their mouths they profess that they do" (Titus 1:16). If they knew the means and the purpose of their creation by God, they would not despise these other stations nor exalt their own so highly; they would recognize the purity of these as the works and creatures of God, and would honor them, willingly remain in them, and be of service to their neighbor. That would be the true recognition of God, both in His Word and in His creatures, and the true purity of both heart and conscience, which comes to this faith and conclusion: whatever God does and ordains must be pure and good. For He makes nothing impure, and He consecrates everything through the Word which He has attached to every station and creature.

Therefore, be on guard against all your own ideas if you want to be pure before God. See to it that your heart is founded and fastened on the Word of God. Then you will be purer than all the Carthusians and saints in the world. When I was young, people used to take pride in this proverb: "Enjoy being alone, and your heart will stay pure."[7] In support of it they would cite a quotation from Saint Bernard, who said that whenever he was among people, he defiled himself. In the lives of the fathers we read about a hermit who would not let anyone

---

[7]This proverb is the first half of a medieval rhyme that Luther was fond of quoting in his criticisms of monasticism.

come near him or talk to him, because, he said, "The angels cannot come to anyone who moves around in human society." We also read about two others, who would not let their mother see them. She kept watch, and once she caught them. Immediately they closed the door and let her stand outside for a long time crying; finally they persuaded her to go away and to wait until they would see each other in the life hereafter.

This is what they call a noble deed, the highest kind of sanctity and the most perfect kind of purity. But what was it really? Here is the Word of God: "Honor your father and your mother" (Exod. 20:12). If they had regarded this as holy and pure, they would have shown their mother and their neighbor all honor, love, and friendship. On the contrary, they followed their own ideas and a holiness they chose for themselves; hence they isolated themselves from them, and by their very effort to be most pure they most shamefully profaned themselves before God. As though even the most desperate scoundrels could not have such thoughts and put on such a show that people would have to say, "These are living saints! They can despise the world and have to do only with angels." With angels all right—from the abyss of hell! The angels like nothing more than to watch us deal with the Word of God; with such people they enjoy dwelling. Therefore, leave the angels up there in heaven undisturbed. Look for them here on earth below, in your neighbor, father and mother, children, and others. Do for these what God has commanded, and the angels will never be far away from you.

I have said this to help people evaluate this matter correctly and not go so far away to look for it as the monks do. They have thrown it out of the world altogether and stuck it into a corner or a cowl. All this is stench and filth and the devil's real dwelling. Let it be where God has put it, in a heart that clings to God's Word and that regards its tasks and every creature on the basis of it. Then the chief purity, that of faith toward God, will also manifest itself outwardly in this life. Everything will proceed from obedience to the Word and command of God, regardless of whether it is physically clean or unclean. I spoke earlier of a judge who has to condemn a man to death, who thus sheds blood and defiles himself with it. A monk would regard this as an abominably impure act, but Scripture says it is the service of God. In Romans 13:4 Paul calls the government, which bears the sword, "God's servant." This is not its own work and command, but His, which He imposes on it and demands from it.

Now you have the meaning of "pure heart": it is one that functions completely on the basis of the pure Word of God. What is their reward; what does He promise to them? "They shall see God." A wonderful title and an excellent treasure! But what does it mean to "see God"? Here again the monks have their own dreams. To them it means sitting in a cell and elevating your thoughts heavenward, leading a "contemplative life," as they call it in the many books they have written about it. That is still a far cry from seeing God, when you come marching along on your own ideas and scramble up to heaven, the way the sophists, schismatic spirits, and crazy saints insist on using their own brains to measure and master God together with His Word and works. But if you have a true faith that Christ is your Savior, then you see immediately that you have a gracious God. For faith leads you up and opens up the heart and will of God for you. There you see sheer, superabundant grace and love. That is exactly what it means "to see God," not with physical eyes, with which no one can see Him in this life, but with faith, which sees His fatherly, friendly heart, where there is no anger or displeasure. Anyone who regards Him as angry is not seeing Him correctly, but has pulled down a curtain and cover, more, a dark cloud over His face. But in scriptural language "to see His face" means to recognize Him correctly as a gracious and faithful Father, on whom you can depend for every good thing. This happens only through faith in Christ.

Therefore, if according to God's Word and command you live in your station with your husband, wife, child, neighbor, or friend, you can see God's intention in these things; and you can come to the conclusion that they please Him, since this is not your own dream, but His Word and command, which never deludes or deceives us. It is a wonderful thing, a treasure beyond every thought or wish, to know that you are standing and living in the right relation to God. In this way not only can your heart take comfort and pride in the assurance of His grace, but you can know that your outward conduct and behavior is pleasing to Him. From this it follows that cheerfully and heartily you can do and suffer anything, without letting it make you fearful or despondent. None of this is possible for those who lack this faith and pure heart guided only by God's Word. Thus, all the monks have publicly taught that no one can know whether or not he is in a state of grace.[8] It serves them right that because they despise faith and true godly works and seek their own purity, they must never see God or know how they stand in relation to Him.

Ask one who has most diligently observed his canoni-

---

[8]At the Council of Trent (Session VI, Canon 16), this was to become the official teaching of the Roman Catholic Church, but in the following form: "If anyone says with absolute and infallible certainty that he will certainly have that great gift of perseverance until the end, unless he teaches this on the basis of special revelation, let him be anathema."

cal hours of prayer, celebrated Mass and fasted daily, whether he is also sure that this is pleasing to God. He must say he does not know, that he is doing it all as a risk: "If it succeeds, let it succeed." It is impossible for anyone to say anything else. None of them can make a boast and say, "God gave me this cowl, He commanded me to wear it, He ordered me to celebrate this Mass." Until now we have all been groping in such blindness as this. We performed many works, contributed, fasted, prayed our rosaries; and yet we never dared to say, "This work is pleasing to God; of this I am sure, and I would be willing to die for it." Hence, no one can boast that in all his life and activity he has ever seen God. Or if in his pride someone glorifies such works and thinks that God must be well disposed to them and reward him for them, he is not seeing God but the devil in place of God. There is no word of God to support him; it is all the invention of men, grown up in their own hearts. That is why it can never assure or pacify any heart, but remain hidden by pride until it comes to its final gasps, when it all disappears and brings on despair, so that one never gets around to seeing the face of God. But anyone who takes hold of the Word of God and who remains in faith can take his stand before God and look at Him as his gracious Father. He does not have to be afraid that He is standing behind him with a club; and he is sure that He is looking at him and smiling graciously, together with all the angels and saints in heaven.

You see, that is what Christ means by this statement, that only those who have such a pure heart see God. By this He cuts off and puts aside every other kind of purity. Where this kind is absent, everything else in a man may be pure; but it is worth nothing before God, and he can never see God. Where the heart is pure, on the other

hand, everything is pure; and it does not matter if outwardly everything is impure, yes, if the body is full of
sores, scabs, and leprosy.

Blessed are the peacemakers, for they shall be called the children of God.

With an excellent title and wonderful praise the Lord
here honors those who do their best to try to make
peace, not only in their own lives but also among other
people, who try to settle ugly and involved issues, who
endure squabbling and try to avoid and prevent war and
bloodshed. This is a great virtue, too, but one that is very
rare in the world and among the counterfeit saints.
Those who are not Christians are both liars and murderers, as is their father, the devil (John 8:44). Therefore,
they have no other goal than to stir up unrest, quarrels,
and war. Thus, among the priests, bishops, and princes
nowadays practically all we find are bloodhounds. They
have given many evidences that there is nothing they
would rather see than all of us swimming in blood. If a
prince loses his temper, he immediately thinks he has to
start a war. Then he inflames and incites everyone, until
there has been so much war and bloodshed that he re-
grets it and gives a few thousand [gold coins] for the
souls that were killed. These are bloodhounds, and that
is what they remain. They cannot rest until they have
taken revenge and spent their anger, until they have
dragged their land and people into misery and sorrow.
Yet they claim to bear the title "Christian princes" and
to have a just cause.

You need more to start a war than having a just cause.
As we have said, this does not prohibit the waging of war;
for Christ has no intention here of taking anything away

from the government and its official authority, but is only teaching individuals who want to lead a Christian life. Still it is not right for a prince to make up his mind to go to war against his neighbor, even though, I say, he has a just cause and his neighbor is in the wrong. The command is "Blessed are the peacemakers." Therefore, anyone who claims to be a Christian and a child of God, not only does not start war or unrest; but he also gives help and counsel on the side of peace wherever he can, even though there may have been a just and adequate cause for going to war. It is sad enough if one has tried everything and nothing helps, and then he has to defend himself, to protect his land and people. Therefore, not "Christians" but "children of the devil" is the name for those quarrelsome young noblemen who immediately draw and unsheathe their sword on account of one word. Even worse are the ones that are now persecuting the Gospel and ordering the burning and murder of innocent preachers of the Gospel, who have done them no harm but only good and have served them with body and soul. We are not talking about these right now, but only about those who claim that they are in the right and have a just cause, thinking that as high and princely personages they ought not to suffer, even though other people do.

This also means that if you are the victim of injustice and violence, you have no right to take the advice of your own foolish head and immediately start getting even and hitting back; but you are to think it over, try to bear it and have peace. If that is impossible and you cannot stand it, you have law and government in the country, from which you can seek legitimate redress. It is ordained to guard against such things and to punish them. Therefore, anyone who does violence to you sins not only against you but also against the government itself; for the order and command to maintain peace was given to the government and not to you. Therefore, leave the vengeance and punishment to your judge, who has the command; it is against him that your enemy has done wrong. If you take it upon yourself to wreak vengeance, you do an even greater wrong. You become guilty of the same sin as he who sins against the government and interferes with its duties, and by doing so you invalidate the justice of your own righteous cause. For the proverb says, "The one who strikes back is in the wrong, and striking back makes a quarrel."[9]

Note that this is one demand that Christ makes here in opposition to those who are vengeful and violent. He gives the name "peacemakers," in the first place, to those who help make peace among lands and people, like pious princes, counselors, or jurists, to people in government who hold their rule and reign for the sake of peace; and in the second place, to pious citizens and neighbors, who with their salutary and good tongues adjust, reconcile, and settle quarrels and tensions between husband and wife or between neighbors, brought on by evil and poisonous tongues. Thus, Saint Augustine boasts that when his mother Monica saw two people at odds, she would always speak the best to both sides. Whatever good she heard about the one, she brought to the other; but whatever evil she heard, that she kept to herself or mitigated as much as possible. In this way she often brought on a reconciliation. It is especially among womenfolk that the shameful vice of slander is prevalent, so that great misfortune is often caused by an evil tongue. This is the work of those bitter and poisonous brides of

---

[9]A proverb cited by Luther.

the devil, who when they hear a word about another, viciously make it sharper, more pointed, and more bitter against the others, so that sometimes misery and murder are the result.

All this comes from the shameful, demonic filth which naturally clings to us, that everyone enjoys hearing and telling the worst about his neighbor and it tickles him to see a fault in someone else. If a woman were as beautiful as the sun but had one little spot or blemish on her body, you would be expected to forget everything else and to look only for that spot and to talk about it. If a lady were famous for her honor and virtue, still some poisonous tongue would come along and say that she had once been seen laughing with some man and defame her in such a way as to eclipse all her praise and honor. These are really poisonous spiders that can suck out nothing but poison from a beautiful, lovely rose, ruining both the flower and the nectar, while a little bee sucks out nothing but honey, leaving the roses unharmed. That is the way some people act. All they can notice about other people are the faults or impurities which they can denounce, but what is good about them they do not see. People have many virtues which the devil cannot destroy, yet he hides or disfigures them to make them invisible. For example, even though a woman may be full of faults and have no other virtue, she is still a creature of God. At least she can carry water and wash clothes. There is no person on earth so bad that he does not have something about him that is praiseworthy. Why is it, then, that we leave the good things out of sight and feast our eyes on the unclean things? It is as though we enjoyed only looking at—if you will pardon the expression—a man's behind, while God has covered the unpresentable parts of the body and, as Paul says, has given them "greater honor" (1 Cor. 12:24). We are so filthy that we only look for what is dirty and stinking, and wallow in it like pigs.

You see, these are also real children of the devil, who gets his name from doing this. He is called *diabolus*, that is, a slanderer and reviler, who takes pleasure in shaming us most miserably and embittering us among ourselves, causing nothing but murder and misery and tolerating no peace or concord between brothers, between neighbors, or between husband and wife. I once heard of a case where a married couple lived together in such love and harmony that it was the talk of the whole town. When the devil was unable to undermine this in any other way, he sent an old hag to the wife, to tell her that her husband was having an affair with another woman and planned to kill her. Thus, she embittered the wife against her husband and advised her to hide a knife on her person in order to beat him to it. When the hag had done this, she went to the husband and told him the same, that his wife planned to murder him; and as proof of it, she said, he would find a knife next to her in bed at night. He found it, and he cut her head off with it. Whether this story is fact or fiction, it does show what such wicked and poisonous mouths can do, even to people who love each other deeply. Thus, they may rightly be called "the devil's mouths" or she-devils; for the devil, *diabolus*, means nothing else than a bitter, poisonous, evil mouth.

So be on your guard against such people, and neither listen nor pay attention to them. Learn to put the best interpretation on what you hear about your neighbor, or even to conceal it, so that you may establish and preserve peace and harmony. Then you can honorably bear the title "child of God" before the whole world and before the angels in heaven. You should let this honor draw and attract you; in fact, you should chase it to the end of the world, if need be, and gladly surrender everything you have for it. Now you have it offered to you here and spread out in front of you for nothing. There is nothing that you have to do or give for it, except that if you want to be a child of God, you must also show yourself to be one and do your Father's works toward your neighbor. This is what Christ, our Lord, has done for us by reconciling us to the Father, bringing us into His favor, daily representing us, and interceding on our behalf.

You do the same. Be a reconciler and a mediator between your neighbors. Carry the best to both sides; but keep quiet about the bad, which the devil has inspired, or explain it the best way you can. If you come to Margaret, do what is said of Monica, Augustine's mother, and say, "My dear Margaret, why are you so bitter? Surely she does not intend it so badly. All I notice about her is that she would like to be your dear sister." In the same way, if you meet Catherine, do the same thing. Then, as a true child of God, you will have made peace on both sides as far as possible.

But if you will or must talk about an evil deed, do as Christ has taught you. Do not carry it to others, but go to the one who has done it, and admonish him to improve. Do not act ostentatiously when you come and expose the person involved, speaking when you ought to be quiet and being quiet when you ought to speak. This is the first method: you should discuss it between yourself and your neighbor alone (Matt. 18:15). If you must tell it to others, however, when the first method does not work, then tell it to those who have the job of punishing, father and mother, master and mistress, burgomaster and judge. That is the right and proper procedure for removing and punishing a wrong. Otherwise, if you spread it among other people, the person remains unimproved; and the wrong remains unpunished, besides being broadcast by you and by others, so that everyone washes out his mouth with it. Look what a faithful physician does with a sick child. He does not run around among the people and broadcast it; but he goes to the child and examines his pulse or anything else that is necessary, not to gratify his pleasure at the cost of the child, nor to make fun of him, but with the good, honest intention of helping him. So we read about that holy patriarch Joseph in Genesis 37. He was tending the cattle with his brothers; and when he heard an evil report about them, he went and brought it to their father as their superior, whose task it was to investigate and to punish them because they would not listen to him.

But you may say, "Then why do you yourself publicly attack the pope and others, instead of keeping the peace?" Answer: A person must advise and support peace while he can and keep quiet as long as possible. But when the sin is evident and becomes too widespread or does public damage, as the pope's teaching has, then there is no longer time to be quiet but only to defend and attack, especially for me and others in public office whose task it is to teach and to warn everyone. I have the commission and charge, as a preacher and a doctor, to see to it that no one is misled, so that I may give account of it at the Last Judgment (Heb. 13:17). So Saint Paul commands the preachers to watch and guard their whole flock against the wolves that were to appear among them (Acts 20:28). Thus, it is my duty to chastise public sinners so that they may improve, just as a judge must publicly condemn and punish evildoers in the performance of his office. As we have said often enough, Christ is not talking here about public office, but in general about all Christians insofar as we are all alike before God.

Blessed are those who are persecuted for righteousness' sake, for theirs is the kingdom of heaven.

I have said earlier that all these items and promises must be understood by faith in reference to things that are neither seen nor heard and that they are not talking about outward appearances. How can the poor and the mourners be said to look outwardly successful and blessed when, in addition, they have to suffer all sorts of persecution—all things that the whole world and our reason calls trouble and that they say should be avoided? Therefore whoever wants to have the blessedness and the possessions that Christ is talking about here, must lift up his heart far above all senses and reason. He must not evaluate himself on the basis of his feelings, but he must argue this way, "If I am poor, then I am not poor. I am poor outwardly, according to the flesh; but before God, in faith, I am rich." Thus when he feels sad, troubled, and worried, he must not use this standard and say that he is not a blessed man. But he must turn himself over and say, "I feel sorrow, misery, and sadness of heart; but still I am blessed, happy, and settled on the basis of the Word of God." The situation in the world is the exact counterpart of this, for those who are called rich and happy are not. Christ calls out His "Woe!" against them and calls them unhappy (Luke 6:24, 25), although it appears that they are well off and having the greatest possible success. Therefore, they should lift up their thoughts above the riches and fun which they are having and say, "Yes, I am rich and living in the midst of pure fun. But too bad for me if I have nothing else; for there must certainly be plenty of trouble, misery, and sorrow in all this that will come over me before I feel it or know it." This applies to all these items; every one of them looks different before the world from the way it looks according to these words.

So far we have been treating almost all the elements of a Christian's way of life and the spiritual fruits under these two headings: first, that in his own person he is poor, troubled, miserable, needy, and hungry; second, that in relation to others he is a useful, kind, merciful, and peaceable man, who does nothing but good works. Now [Christ] adds the last: how he fares in all this. Although he is full of good works, even toward his enemies and rascals, for all this he must get this reward from the world: he is persecuted and runs the risk of losing his body, his life, and everything.

If you want to be a Christian, therefore, consider this well, lest you be frightened, lose heart, and become impatient. But be cheerful and content, knowing that you are not badly off when this happens to you. [Christ] and all the saints had the same experience, as He says a little later. For this reason He issues a warning beforehand to those who want to be Christians, that they should and must suffer persecution. Therefore you may take your choice. You have two ways before you—either to heaven and eternal life or to hell; either with Christ or with the world. But this you must know: if you live in order to have a good time here without persecution, then you will not get to heaven with Christ, and vice versa. In short, you must either surrender Christ and heaven, or make up your mind that you are willing to suffer every kind of persecution and torture in the world. Briefly, anyone who wants to have Christ must put in jeopardy his body, life, goods, reputation, and popularity in the world. He dare not let himself be scared off by contempt, ingratitude, or persecution.

The reason is this: the devil is a wicked and angry spirit. He will not and cannot stand seeing a man enter the kingdom of God. And if the man undertakes to do so, he blocks the way himself, arousing and attempting every kind of opposition he can summon. If you want to be God's child, therefore, prepare yourself for persecution, as the wise man says.[10] Paul says in 2 Timothy 3:12, "All who desire to live a godly life in Christ Jesus will be persecuted." And Christ Himself says, "The disciple should not be better off than his master. If they persecuted Me, they will also persecute you" (John 15:20). There is no other way out, and therefore, "Blessed are those who are persecuted for the sake of the kingdom of heaven," to let us know how to console ourselves. Otherwise, this would look outwardly like a troubling and unhappy situation, and it wears us down to be sitting constantly amid danger to life and property. But when faith takes over, we can lift ourselves up above this and think, "Nevertheless, Christ has said that I am blessed and well off. Because He has said so, I let it be my comfort and pleasure. The Word will make my heart great, yes, greater than heaven and earth. What are all my persecutors in comparison with this Man or His Word? If there are one or two persecuting us, there are many more (2 Kings 6:16) defending us, cheering us up, consoling us, and blessing us—yes, ten thousand angels over against one of them, together with all the saints, who act in concert with Christ and with God Himself." Hence,

---

[10]This appears to be a reference to John 15:20, which is explicitly quoted a few lines further; of course, the passage itself may have had a proverbial background.

we must not be so coarse and cold, letting this Word lie around, but blow it up and magnify it, pitting it against every persecution. Then we shall see and learn that we should despise all our suffering as nothing at all when compared with this great consolation and eternal blessing.

But it is significant that He should add the phrase, "for righteousness' sake," to show that where this condition is absent, persecution alone will not accomplish this. The devil and wicked people also have to suffer persecution. Rascals often get into each other's hair, and there is no love lost between them. So one murderer persecutes another, and the Turk battles against the Tartar; but this does not make them blessed. This statement applies only to those who are persecuted for righteousness' sake. So also 1 Peter 4:15 says, "Let none of you suffer as a murderer or a thief or a wrongdoer." Therefore, bragging and yelling about great suffering is worthless without this condition. So the godless monks have deceived the poor people whom they have led away to be punished, consoling them with the statement that with their death they were paying for their sins. Beware of any death that is supposed to pay for your sin, for it belongs in the abyss of hell. First there must come righteousness and the death of Christ the Lord.

See to it, therefore, that you have a genuine divine cause for whose sake you suffer persecution, and that you are really convinced of it so that your conscience can take a stand and stick by it, even though the whole world should stand up against you. The primary thing is that you grasp the Word of God firmly and surely so that there can be no doubt or hesitation there. Suppose that the emperor, the bishops, or the princes were to forbid marriage, freedom in the choice of food, the use of both

kinds in the sacrament, and the like, and were to persecute you for these things. Then you would have to see to
it that your heart is convinced and persuaded that the
Word of God has made these things free and unprohib-
ited, that it even commands us to take them seriously
and to stake our lives upon them. Then you can have the
confidence to say, "This cause does not belong to me but
to Christ, my Lord. For I have not concocted it out of my
own head. I have not assumed or begun it on my own or
at the advice or suggestion of any man. But it has been
brought and announced to me from heaven through the
mouth of Christ, who never deludes or deceives me but
is Himself sheer truth and righteousness. At this Man's
Word I will take the risk of suffering, of doing and for-
saking whatever I should. All by itself, His Word will accomplish more to comfort and strengthen my heart than
the raging and threatening of all the devils and of the
world can accomplish to frighten me."

Who cares if a crazy prince or foolish emperor fumes
in his rage and threatens me with sword, fire, or the gallows! Just as long as my Christ is talking dearly to my
heart, comforting me with the promises that I am
blessed, that I am right with God in heaven, and that all
the heavenly host and creation called me blessed. Just let
my heart and mind be ready to suffer for the sake of His
Word and work. Then why should I let myself be scared
by these miserable people, who rage and foam in their
hostility to God but suddenly disappear like a puff of
smoke or a bubble, as the prophet Isaiah says, "I, I am
He that comforts you; who are you that you are afraid of
man who dies, of the son of man who is made like grass,
and have forgotten the Lord, who made you, who
stretched out the heavens and laid the foundations of the
earth?" (Isa. 51:12, 13). That is to say, "He who comforts

you and takes pleasure in you is almighty and eternal. When it is all over with them, He will still be sitting up there, and so will you. Why, then, let the threatening and fuming of a miserable, stinking bag of worms concern you more than this divine comfort and approval? Be grateful to God and happy in your heart that you are worthy of suffering this, as the apostles went forth leaping for joy over the fact that they were disgraced and beaten down (Acts 5:41).

You see, these words are a great blessing to us if only we receive them with love and thanks, since we have no shortage of persecution. But our great advantage is that our enemies themselves cannot condemn our cause and must acknowledge—no thanks to them!—that it is right and true. What is wrong is the fact that we are teaching it, for they refuse to learn or accept it from us. Such a thing is unprecedented and unheard of. What we suffer on this account, therefore, is a holy and blessed suffering, as they themselves must testify. This is no longer a human persecution, but a truly demonic one, when they say that we must not and dare not call it the Word of God but must keep our mouths shut and not preach unless first we go and fall at the pope's feet, asking for approval from him and from his masks.

So let us be all the more willing and happy to suffer everything they can do against us, since we have the strong and certain comfort and the great and glorious satisfaction that their own mouth confirms our teaching and our cause. In addition, we hear the wonderful and delightful promise here that we shall be well rewarded in heaven and that we should be happy and rejoice over this, as people who do not have to yearn for heaven but already have it. All they do by their persecution is to further this, actually driving and chasing us to heaven. Now tell me whether these simple, short words do not encourage you as much as the whole world can, and provide more comfort and joy than all the suffering and torture our enemies can inflict on us. We should not listen to them with only *half* an ear, but take them to heart and ponder them.

This applies to persecution with deeds and fists, involving person or property, when Christians are seized and tortured, burned, hanged, and massacred, as happens nowadays and has happened before. There is, in addition, another kind of persecution. It is called defamation, slander, or disgrace, involving our reputation and good name. In this way Christians have to suffer more than others. Now Christ discusses this.

Blessed are you when men revile you and persecute you and utter all kinds of evil against you falsely on My account.

This, too, is a great persecution and, as I have said, the real suffering of Christians, that they endure bitter slander and poisonous defamation. Though other people must also suffer persecution, violent and unjust treatment, still men are willing to let them keep their reputation and good name. So this is not yet really Christian suffering, which requires not merely all sorts of tortures and troubles, but more; their good name must be spit upon and slandered, and the world must boast loudly that in murdering the Christians it has executed the worst kind of criminal, whom the earth could no longer carry, and that it has done God the greatest and most acceptable service, as Christ says (John 16:2). Thus no name has ever appeared on earth so slanderous and disreputable as the name "Christian." No nation has ever experienced so much bitter opposition and attack by wicked and poisonous tongues as have the Christians.

Right now they are proving this in the slander, defamation, lies, deceit, vicious tricks, and wicked misinterpretations they have perpetrated against the dear gospel and its preachers, such that one would die many times rather than endure these poisonous, malicious darts (Eph. 6:16). Along comes the pope with his thunderbolts, damning us to the ninth hell as the children of the devil. In the same way his retinue, the bishops and princes, rage and roar with such terrible blasphemies and slanders that our whole body trembles, and we would soon tire and give up if we did not have a comfort stronger and more powerful than all their malice and rage. Thus, we let them rage and blaspheme. They will only plague themselves, and their poisonous hatred and insatiable envy will give them a burning pain. But we are content and courageous. If they want to rage and storm, we can still laugh and be joyful.

Therefore, I say it again: anyone who wants to be a Christian should learn to expect such persecution from poisonous, evil, slanderous tongues, especially when they cannot do anything with their fists. He should let the whole world sharpen its tongue on him, aim at him, sting and bite. Meanwhile, he should regard all this with defiant contempt and laughter in God's name, letting them rage in the name of their god, the devil, and being firmly persuaded, as we have said above, that our cause is the right cause and is God's own cause. [Even] they [must] confirm [this;] even though they condemn us, they have to say it is the truth. Besides, before God our hearts and consciences are sure that our teaching is right. We are not teaching on the basis of our own brains, reason, or wisdom, or using this to gain advantage, property, or reputation for ourselves before the world. We are preaching only God's Word and praising only His deeds. Our enemies, on the other hand, brag about nothing but their own deeds, merits, and holiness. They persecute us for refusing to join them in this.

They do not persecute us for being adulterers, robbers, or thieves. In fact, they can tolerate the most desperate scoundrels and criminals in their midst. But they are raising such a hue and cry because we refuse to approve their teaching and life, because we praise nothing but the gospel, Christ, faith, and truly good works, and because we do not suffer for ourselves but suffer everything for the sake of Christ the Lord. Therefore, we will sing it to the end with them. No matter how hard their head, ours is still harder. In short, they must let that Man alone, whether they like it or not.

Rejoice and be glad, for your reward is great in heaven.

These are really sweet and comforting words. They should gladden and encourage our hearts against all kinds of persecution. Should not the dear Lord's Word and comfort be dearer and more important to us than that which comes from a helpless bag of worms, or the rage, threats, excommunication, curses, and lightning of the miserable pope, even though he deluged us with the very dregs and the whole hell of his wrath and cursing? For I hear my Lord Christ telling me that He is truly delighted, and commanding me to be happy about it. In addition, He promises me such a wonderful reward: the kingdom of heaven shall be mine and everything that Christ has, together with all the saints and all Christendom—in short, such a treasure and comfort that I should not trade it for all the possessions, joy, and music in the whole world, even though all the leaves and all the blades of grass were tongues singing my praises. This is not a Christian calling me "blessed," nor even an angel, but the Lord of all the angels, before whom they and all the creatures must kneel and adore. With all the other creatures, therefore, with the leaves and the grass, they must cheerfully sing and dance in my honor and praise.

And those who slander and curse me, what are they by comparison but nits and lousy paunches—if you will pardon the expression—so shameful that there is no name for them. If every creature, the leaves and the blades of grass in the forest, and the sand on the shore were all tongues to accuse and destroy them, what would all that be in comparison with a single word of this Man? His voice sounds clear enough to fill heaven and earth and to echo through them, silencing the slobbering coughs and the hoarse scratching of His enemies.

You see, that is how we should learn something about using these words for our benefit. They are not put here for nothing but were spoken and written for our strengthening and comfort. By them our dear Master and faithful Shepherd, or Bishop, arms us. Then we shall be unafraid and ready to suffer if for His sake they lay all kinds of torment and trouble upon us in both words and deeds, and we shall despise whatever is offensive to us, even though contrary to our own reason and heart.

For if we cling to our own thoughts and feelings, we are dismayed and hurt to learn that for our service, help, counsel, and kindness to the world and to everyone we should get no thanks except the deepest and bitterest hatred and cursed, poisonous tongues. If flesh and blood were in charge here, it would soon say, "If I am to get nothing else out of this, then let anyone who wants to, stick with the gospel and be a Christian! The world can go to the devil for help if that is what it wants!" This is the reason for the general complaint and cry that the gospel is causing so much conflict, strife, and disturbance in the world and that everything is worse since it came than it was before, when things moved along smoothly, when there was no persecution, and when the people lived together like good friends and neighbors.

But it says, "If you do not want to have the gospel or be a Christian, then go out and take the world's side. Then you will be its friend, and no one will persecute you. But if you want to have the gospel and Christ, then you must count on having trouble, conflict, and persecution wherever you go." The devil cannot bear it otherwise, nor will he stop egging people on against the gospel, so that all the world is incensed against it. Thus, at the present time peasants, city people, nobles, princes, and lords oppose the gospel from sheer cussedness, and even they do not know why.

So I say in reply to these idle talkers and grumblers, "Things neither can nor should run peacefully and smoothly. How could things run smoothly, when the devil is in charge, and is a mortal enemy of the gospel? There is good reason for this, too, since it hurts him in his kingdom, where he can feel it. If he were to let it go ahead unhindered, it would soon be all over and his kingdom would be utterly destroyed. But if he is to resist it and hinder it, he must rally all his art and power and arouse everything in his might against it. So do not hope for any peace and quiet so long as Christ and His gospel are in the midst of the devil's kingdom. And woe upon the peaceful and smooth situation that used to be, and upon those who would like to have it back! This is a sure sign that the devil is ruling with all his might and that no Christ is there. I am worried that it may be this way again and that the gospel may be taken away from us Germans all too soon, which is just what these rioters are struggling for now."

But we have the assurance that it is not our fault when there is trouble. It would give us heartfelt joy if everything went right. We have done our share. We have been teaching, warning, pleading, beseeching, and giving in, even to our enemies, offering them peace, and doing everything we should do. We have given help and counsel with all our might, at our own risk and disadvantage, tolerating what we should. Yet all we accomplish is shameful and poisonous persecution, slander, and abuse from men who will not stop till they have cooled their rage in our blood. Since the situation will never be different, we let them go ahead with their threatenings, fury, and blasphemy, and hold on to the comfort we have heard. We are sure that they cannot accomplish what they desire until they first topple Christ from heaven and make a liar out of Him, with all that He has said.

For Martin Luther the message of the gospel is the most glorious of all messages. It is the promise of God's love for man and His provision for his salvation. Luther's sermon on John 3:16 is rich in content. Any reader who desires to know the essence of the gospel will find an unsurpassed explanation in this fine message. Luther describes clearly the Incarnation, showing that Jesus was not two persons, but two natures—one human and one divine—in one person. He emphasizes that Christ was sent as the sacrifice for our sins and through His death the curse of death has been defeated. We appropriate the gift of God by believing in the Lord Jesus Christ. This, as Luther explains, is the gospel: We are made sons of God by faith alone.

CHAPTER FIVE

John 3:16

For God so loved the world.

Shortly before, Christ had said, "The Son of man must be lifted up, that whoever believes in Him may have eternal life." Now He says, "God so loved the world that He gave His only Son, that whoever believes in Him should not perish but have eternal life." What Christ said about the Son of man—that He must be lifted up— He now also says about the Son of God. He tells us that God's great love prompted Him to give His only Son. Earlier He said that Mary had given her Son, and now He says, "God the Father gave His Son to be crucified." God's Son and Mary's Son is only one Person. He appropriates both natures for the work of salvation and redemption from eternal death. John the evangelist always links the two natures, deity and humanity, together.

Someone may ask, "How is it possible for the Son of

man to save and to give eternal life?" Or, "How can it be that God's Son should be delivered to be crucified?" It sounds plausible that the Son of man might be crucified, but that He should bestow eternal life does not seem reasonable. And it seems just as incongruous that God's Son should die and give His life for the life of the world. But we must bear in mind that when we speak of Christ, we are thinking of His two natures in one person and that what is ascribed to the two natures is really comprehended in one person. Thus, I can very properly say that the Son of man created heaven and earth, just as I say that the Son of God is the Creator of heaven and earth. We dare not follow those heretics, the Nestorians, the ancestors of the Turks,[1] who alleged that only Mary's Son, not God's Son, died for us. For here we find it clearly stated and written, "God gave His Son for the world." And this Son is assuredly not only Mary's Son, born of Mary, but also the Son of God. And when Christ was delivered to Pilate to be crucified, and when Pilate led Him from the judgment hall, he took hold of the hand not only of the man Jesus but also of the Son of God, whom he crucified. Therefore, Saint Paul said, "If they had understood, they would not have crucified the King of glory" (1 Cor. 2:8), whom all creatures usually adore. Thus, it was God's Son who was conceived by the Virgin Mary, who suffered and died, was buried, descended into hell, and rose again from the dead.

This is the way to interpret expressions of the apostles, bishops, and ancient teachers, "Oh, Thou Son of David!" Or, "Thou Son of Mary, have mercy on me!" "Oh, dear Jesus, born of the Virgin Mary, be gracious to me!" The

---

[1] Nestorian Christians were indeed among those with whom Mohammed came into contact in his formative years. The Moslems also came into contact with Nestorians in Persia in the seventh century.

words are a prayer to God and are the equivalent of, "Oh, Jesus, Thou Son of God, have mercy on me!" In these words you also worship the Son of Mary, because the two natures are united in the one Christ.

Thus, the words of this text indicate that God gave His Son for us and that the Son of man died for us. There are not two Jesuses, the one coming from the Father and the other born of Mary. No, there is only one Jesus. Therefore, the ancient fathers said that the attributes of both natures are ascribed and imputed to the whole person of Christ "in the concrete," creating a "communication of properties," a union in which the attributes of the one nature are imparted to the other. Each nature, of course, has its own peculiar character. For instance, it is peculiar to the human nature of Christ to be born of the Virgin Mary. The divine nature has different attributes. But since the person of Christ cannot be divided, there is a communion, which enables one to say, "The infant Christ, who lies in the cradle and is suckled by the Virgin Mary, created heaven and earth." Also, "The Son of God who is with the Father from eternity nurses at His mother's breasts, is crucified, and dies." "For the communion of the natures also effects a communication of properties." The ancient fathers diligently taught this and wrote about it.

But now we have to make the practical application and learn why the person who is God and man came into the world. The Lord Christ teaches us this too, when He says that any believer in Him shall be delivered from eternal death and be assured of eternal life. It was not an angel, a principality, or any of the world's mighty who became incarnate and died for us—no, both the angelic and the human nature would have been too weak—but it was the divine nature that assumed humanity. It was Christ who adopted our flesh and blood that we might be saved through Him.

Now we see how gloriously the evangelist John speaks of Christ and of the sublime doctrine of our Christian faith: that Christ is both God and man. This is what John stresses in his Gospel. He says nothing about the necessity of good works for salvation, as the wicked pope does.

The Lord informed Nicodemus in an excellent sermon that no one will go to heaven or enter the kingdom of God unless he is born anew and believes in the serpent hanging on the cross, that is, believes in the Son of man, who was lifted up that all who believe in Him should not perish but have everlasting life. This is the new spiritual birth, the way to eternal life, namely, faith in the crucified Son of man. Now Christ stresses, and enlarges on, this theme in the fine sermon delivered to only one man, Nicodemus. It seems surprising that He should preach so beautifully to him. Yet His sermon is not in vain; it awakens in Nicodemus a love for Christ which does not only endure during the lifetime of Christ but lives on after His death (John 19:39). The end and aim of this sermon by Christ is the conversion of Nicodemus. The words, "For God so loved the world" do not need a lengthy commentary and exposition, for we preach on this text every year. Therefore our discussion will be brief.

After Christ has said, "As Moses lifted up the serpent in the wilderness, so must the Son of man be lifted up," He continues with the words, "For God so loved the world, that He gave His only Son, that whoever believes in Him should not perish but have eternal life." To astound Nicodemus, He repeats what He had said before.

As though He wanted to say, "Dear Nicodemus, is it not wonderful that the Son of man is hanged on the cross and lifted up, and that the Son of man, born of the Virgin Mary, true man with body and soul, is also the Son of God? Is it not a miracle that the Son of man and the Son of God are both one Son? (For Christ relates the statement that whosoever believes in Him should not perish but have everlasting life to the Son of man and to the Son of God; this refers to both.) Thus, Nicodemus, I am preaching to you about very important matters which may well astonish you; for instance, about the necessity of the new birth. But still more amazing than this is the process of the new birth." It is, of course, out of the question for a man to re-enter his mother's womb to be born again. No, this is the procedure: God gave His only Son into death for us; that is how we are reborn. Does it not surprise you that for the sake of this rebirth God adopts such a wonderful plan and chooses His only Son—for He has no other—and lets Him become man, instead of selecting some angel or some patriarch? God does not confine Himself to giving us His Son in His incarnation, but He also delivers Him into death for us. He has Him lifted up as Moses lifted up the serpent. Isn't that wonderful? Isn't that medicine effective enough? Who would ever have had the boldness to ask for such a cure for death and sin? But such strong help and powerful medicine will work this for you.

Now you do not understand all this, and you are wondering about this demand for a new birth and about this deliverance from sin. You know full well that we are sinners and are lodged in the jaws of death. Hence, it must sound odd and strange to you that we are to conquer sin and death and need not fear God's stern judgment and

His wrath. Yes indeed, it is strange. But now behold! What is God's plan? The answer would never have occurred to you.

He gave His Son.

Because of His divine wisdom, counsel, and mercy God gives His only begotten Son, who is also the Son of man, as a remedy against sin, death, and your old nature and birth. The Son is "given" to us by dying for us and being buried for us. That, I take it, is another miracle and one far greater. If you are astonished and regard it as incredible that a man must be born anew, this greater wonder must amaze you still more. God loved a poor sinner so much that He gave him, not an angel or a prophet but His only Son. The way of His giving was that His Son became man, and the purpose of His giving was that He might be crucified. This you must learn; and after you have learned it and beheld these wonderful things, your heart will feel constrained to say, "This is truly miraculous! How is it possible?" But if you can accept and believe it, you will conclude, "After all, if God's Son is the cure and remedy for sin and death, why should I be surprised, since I know that God's Son is greater than sin, the devil, and my death?" Just believe it, and you will experience that He is greater. It is surely true that by my own strength I cannot banish death but must die even if I don a monk's cowl, join all the monastic orders and abide by their rules, go on pilgrimages, and perform all those good works on which they place their reliance. None of this is the correct prescription or medicine. But if I can believe in and accept this remedy, that God gives us His Son—not an ordinary son like Abraham, Isaac, and David, of whom God has many, but His only begotten Son—it is certain that this Son can effect a new birth in us and can, therefore, be a victor and conqueror of the devil. This is because God's Son is vastly greater than death, far stronger than sin and the devil. Through Him we have the grace of God rather than wrath, and whatever else we may need besides. If it puzzles you how a man is to be transferred from the devil's realm to the kingdom of God, God's gift of His Son must surprise you still more. And if you accept this in faith, you will no longer be puzzled about the other. If we have the Son of God, who faces death and opposes the devil on our behalf, on our side, let the devil rage as he will. If the Son of God died for me, let death consume and devour me; for he will surely have to return and restore me, and I will stand my ground against him. Christ died; death devoured the Son of God. But in doing so death swallowed a thorn and had to get rid of it. It was impossible for death to hold Him. For this person is God; and since both God and man in one indivisible person entered into the belly of death and the devil, death ate a morsel that ripped [its] stomach open.

It was the counsel of God the Father from eternity to destroy death, ruin the kingdom of the devil, and give the devil a little pill which he would gleefully devour, but which would create a great rumpus in his belly and in the world. Now the Lord wants to say, "Dear Nicodemus, it is miraculous, as you see, that God should spend such a great and precious treasure for our rebirth. For is it a miracle that I, the Son of man and the Son of God in one person, am sacrificed to death and enter the jaws of death and the devil? But I shall not remain there. Not only will I come forth again, but I will also rip open death's belly; for the poison is too potent, and death itself must die."

Christ wants to prevent us from thinking of Him as separate from the Father. Therefore He again directs our mind from Himself to the Father and says that the Father's love for us is just as strong and profound as His own, which is reflected in His sacrificial death. He wants to say, "Whoever beholds the Father's love also beholds Mine; for Our love is identical. I love you with a love that redeems you from sin and death. And the Father's love, which gave you His only Son, is just as miraculous."

Furthermore, Christ tells us how He destroys death and how I am rescued from death. He will be death's venom. Death and [the] law, to be sure, will condemn Him. Therefore, He will have to die and be buried. But He will rise again from the dead. And where He is now, the devil will have to retreat. But how do I approach this Savior and Redeemer? By means of cowls or monastic orders and rules? No! Just cling to the Son in faith. He conquered death and the devil, and He slit the devil's belly open. He will reign and rule again, even though He was crucified under Annas and Caiaphas. Therefore, attach yourself to Him, and you will tear through death and devil; for this text assures us, "Whoever believes in Him shall have eternal life." Accept the truth of this miracle of God's love for the world, and say, "I believe in the Son of God and of Mary, who was lifted up and nailed to the cross." Then you will experience the new birth; for death and sin will no longer accuse, harm, and injure you. Whoever believes in the Son will have eternal life. Cling to His neck or to His garment; that is, believe that He became man and suffered for you. Cross yourself and say, "I am a Christian and will conquer." And you will find that death is vanquished. In Acts 2:24 Saint Peter says that death was not able to hold Christ, since deity and humanity were united in one person. In the same way we, too, shall not remain in death; we shall destroy death, but only if we remain steadfast in faith and cling to death's Destroyer.

In John 17:11 Christ prays, "That they may be one in Me, as I and the Father are one." If I cling to Christ in true faith and remain in Him, it is impossible for sin and death to accuse and condemn me; for Christ has conquered them. This, however, is accomplished, not by our strength but by faith in Him. In this way we, like pious lambs, remain resting in the arms of Christ, the faithful Shepherd.

Therefore, whoever is a Christian and takes hold of Christ by faith is not terrified by the devil; nor is he cowed by sin and death. Even though he feels his sins and is frightened and saddened by them, he nevertheless overcomes this feeling and is not subdued; for he will be quick to say, "I believe in the Son of God and of Mary. He is the devil's venom and death; but at the same time He is my salvation, my remedy, and my life."

We read an excellent story about a certain nun. (In every station of life God preserves some, keeps them in faith, and saves them.) This nun was very much troubled and assaulted by thoughts of the devil and of sin. Of course, all but those who serve their own belly feel God's wrath and judgment; this accounts for the fact that people will take refuge in the saints. Now, since this little nun was filled with terror at the thought of the wrath of God and wanted to be saved, she made it a habit to say whenever the devil troubled her, "Devil, let me alone. I am a Christian!" And the devil had to leave her. On the surface this seems to be a simple technique and easy to learn. But it is necessary that the words be inspired by faith, as those of this little nun were. For the devil did not particularly fear the words, "I am a Christian." No, it was her faith, the fact that she firmly relied on Christ and said, "I am baptized on Christ, and I entrust myself solely to Him; for He is my life, salvation, and wisdom." Wherever such words proceed from faith, they generate a completely fiery atmosphere, which burns and pains the devil so that he cannot tarry. But if a person speaks without warmth about matters pertaining to God and salvation, as the common man does, then the devil merely laughs. But if your words are aglow in your heart, you will put the devil to flight. For then Christ is present. As we read in Hosea 13:14, "He devours death and destroys it"; and here He declares, "Whoever believes in Me shall not perish but have everlasting life." If the believer is to have eternal life, it is implied that he is also free from sin and death. When the devil hears the name of Christ, he flees, because he cannot bear it. But if he does not feel the presence of Him who has destroyed him, he casts man into hell.

I am saying this for the sake of those who think that the mere recital of the words suffices, without any faith in the heart. Thus, many hear these words spoken and also resolve to use them on occasion. I want to tell you a story about this. An ungodly medical doctor in Italy was once asked to stand as godfather for an infant. During the rite of baptism he heard the beautiful words of institution, how the infant became an heir of salvation through Christ, and how the church implored God that Christ would accept this infant. After the baptism, when he pondered these words at home, he became very sad and depressed. As it happened, he had invited guests to dine with him that evening. When the guests noticed his melancholy mood, they asked him why he sighed and why he seemed so troubled in his mind. Then he revealed his feelings and said, "I stood as godfather today and heard some great and wonderful words. If I had the assurance that I was baptized in the same way, I would never again be terrified by the devil." One of the guests was an old man who had actually been godfather at this doctor's baptism. He spoke up, "Now my dear doctor, my dear doctor, you need not be in doubt on that score. For I was present in your baptism. I stood as godfather for you, and I can testify that you, too, were baptized this way." This made the doctor very happy. A little later he rose from the table and went to his room. There he noticed two large, long goat's horns projecting from a wall that had previously been bare. In an attempt to torment the doctor, the devil had assumed the guise of these horns. Now, when the doctor saw this, the thought flashed to him, "But I am baptized; I am a Christian. So why should I fear the devil?" Armed with that faith, he rushed to the wall and broke off one of the horns. Then he hurried back to his guests and joyfully related to them what had happened in the room. The guests all arose from the table and hurried into his room to see whether the one horn was still visible. Lo and behold, they found two horns again protruding from the wall. One of the guests wanted to show off and imitate his host. He said, "Well, I am a Christian too!" And with these words he dashed toward the wall, intending to break off one of the horns. The devil broke his neck and killed him. This guest [had] tried to make light of the whole matter to deck himself with glory. In consequence, his head was torn off, whereas the doctor, who took recourse to faith in the hour of trial, suffered no harm.

This story is undoubtedly credible. My purpose in narrating it is to impress the fact that one must learn not only to recite the words of holy Scripture by rote but also to believe them with one's heart and to remain steadfast in times of peril and in the hour of death. For there are many who speak the words, "I am a Christian," with their mouth but do not believe this in their heart. When trouble besets you, you will find out whether you take these words seriously. In days of sorrow take hold of the Word of God and of faith; pray, and say very fervently, "I am a Christian!" Then you will discover whether you really believe. When a person is not oppressed by sorrow, he has no occasion to perceive this. Callous people, who are not assailed by trouble or temptation, know nothing of this. The rebirth of which Christ speaks here is not acquired while dozing idly and comfortably behind the stove. If you are a Christian and really believe, join the nun in her words, "I am a Christian!" What is the result? You will find relief, and your mind will be at ease; and you will be able to thank God that the devil had to take to his heels. For he cannot withstand these words of fire.

Thus, it all depends on this great and grand miracle, that I believe that God gave His Son for us. If I do not doubt this, then I am able to say in the midst of my trials, "I concede, devil, that I am a sinner burdened with the old Adam and subject to the wrath of God. But what do you, devil, say about this: God so loved the world that He gave His only Son that all who believe in Him might not perish but have eternal life? These words I believe!" And you must speak these words in sincere faith. For Christ has passed through death and sin, and death was power-less to hold Him. And now Christ says, "If you believe in Me, death shall not devour you either. Even if death should hold you for three days or so, as he detained Me for three days in the earth and Jonah for three days in the belly of the whale, he shall nonetheless spew you out again." You might have reason to be surprised about all this—not only that you must be born anew but also that God so loved the world that He gave us a potent plaster, remedy, and syrup against sin, death, the devil, and hell, so that whoever lays that on his heart will not perish.

On the other hand, consider the abominable error of those who directed us to other methods, telling people, for instance, that they should retire into the desert, enter cloisters, or go on pilgrimages—and all this so that we might not perish but have eternal life. I, too, entered the monastery that I might not perish but have eternal life.[2] I wanted to follow my own counsel and help myself by means of the cowl. Truly, it is a vexing and troublesome business. In Turkey and in the papacy this doctrine is still rampant; the Jews teach the same thing. But it really comes from the mouth of the devil.

One might be tempted to ask, "Is it possible that so many can be mistaken about this?" The answer is that the Son of God is stronger than all the gates of hell (Matt. 16:18), also greater than all the monks and their cowls. Nicodemus, too, was curious to hear how he was to be reborn and saved from death. He asked how this was to happen. Jesus told him, "This is the way: the Son of man must be lifted up, and God's Son must be given into death, and man must believe in Him." Even if the world were to teem with monk's cowls and with monastic rules, even if the world were full of the ordinances of the pope, the Turks' Koran, or the Jews' laws, Christ would still be greater than all these. For He is still the Creator of heaven and earth and Lord over all creatures. His sacrifice for me was not Saint Francis or any other monk or the mother of Christ or Saint Peter or an angel or cowls

---

[2]Luther entered the monastery on July 17, 1505.

and tonsures; it was a far more precious treasure. Salvation and deliverance from death call for a greater service than any human or any angel could render. Only God's only begotten Son can render it. The Son swallows up death.

Our adversaries also read this text, but they do not understand it. We also had these words in the papacy, but we failed to comprehend them. Instead, our thoughts were directed solely to our works. And yet some took hold of these words in faith and were saved, like the nun who said, "I am a Christian." I once saw a monk who took a cross into his hands and remarked while the other monks were boasting of their good works, "I know of no merit of my own but only of the merit of Him who died for me on the cross." And in reliance on that merit he also died. In the papacy it was customary to admonish a dying monk to be mindful of his own merits and works and of those of others. And in that faith they died. But just as the pious monk died a blessed death, relying solely on the merit of Jesus Christ, so many a wretched criminal on the gallows has been delivered from sin and saved through faith.

That is how Saint Bernard was saved. He was an exemplary monk; he observed the rules of his order scrupulously, and he fasted so assiduously that his breath stank and no one could abide his presence. But on the threshold of death he exclaimed, "Oh, I have lived damnably! But heavenly Father, Thou hast given me Thy Son, who has a twofold claim to heaven: first, from eternity, by reason of the fact that He is Thy Son; secondly, He earned heaven as the Son of man with His suffering, death, and resurrection. And thus He has also given and bestowed heaven on me." Thereby, Saint Bernard dropped out of the monastic role, forsook cowl and tonsure and rules, and turned to Christ; for he knew that Christ conquered death, not for Himself but for us men, that all who believe in the Son should not perish but have eternal life. And so Saint Bernard was saved.

These are golden words which must be preserved in Christendom; they alone make a person a Christian. You see how woefully those err who try to escape eternal damnation by means of their monkeries, cowls, and tonsures. Moreover, such people even offer their supererogatory works for sale and transfer them to others. This, I regret to say, is how we lived in the papacy. You young people, be grateful to God for your better insight, and learn these words well. For death and the devil are in league with the pope and with the Turks' Koran to delude the people into relying on their foul works for salvation. But salvation demands more than our good works; for not even the holiness of the angels sufficed. God's own Son had to be given to conquer death. Now heaven and the victory over death are not Christ's alone; whoever believes in Him is not to perish but shall have eternal life. On the other hand, whoever refuses to believe is eternally beyond help and rescue, as Christ points out later when He says, "He who does not believe is condemned already" (John 3:18).

Christ said to Nicodemus, "God so loved the world." Furthermore, He assured him that God did not send His Son to condemn the world. From these words we learned that God's Son and the Son of man are one person. We learned that the Son of man was hanged and lifted up as the serpent in the wilderness had been lifted up. This applies properly only to His human nature, since God cannot suffer and be crucified. And yet Christ says here that the Son of God was given into death and was crucified. From this we learn about the "communication of properties," the fact that the attributes of both natures pertain to the one person, that the attributes of both natures inhere in the one person. Despite the fact that Creator and creature are two disparate beings, as different from each other as nothing is from something or from everything, or as different as heaven and earth, still it is true that here they are united.

I am stressing this for a very good reason. Many heretics have arisen—and still more schismatic spirits will appear—who have assailed this article of faith and have been offended at the thought that God should suffer. The Godhead, they argued, is an eternal majesty, while humankind is only a temporal creature. They toyed with this article regarding the two natures in Christ most adroitly and alleged that Mary was not the mother of the Son of God, and that Christ, Mary's Son, is not the Son of God. They were offended by the two natures found in Christ. In place of the two natures they contrived to find two persons. According to holy Scripture, however, we declare that there are two natures in Christ but only one person and not two, and that this one person, God and man, suffered, that the Son of God and of Mary was crucified. A schismatic spirit may contradict this and say, "Ah, God cannot be crucified!" But tell them that this person, who is God and man, was crucified. Since God manages to harmonize this, we, of course, must harmonize it too and declare that Mary is Christ's mother not only according to His humanity, but that she is also the mother of the Son of God and that her Son is both God and man. This is the language Saint Paul employs in Hebrews 6:6, when he speaks of the false Christians who "crucify the Son of God on their own account and hold Him up to contempt." And in 1 Corinthians 2:8 he says, "If they had understood, they would not have crucified the Lord of glory." Since it is the language of Saint Paul and of holy Scripture that the Son of God and the King of glory was crucified, we can accept it without hesitation. Anyone who believes the Bible will not mutter a sound against it. We can also reverse the picture and say, "This Infant, born of Mary and suckled by her or lying in her lap, created heaven and earth." If someone were to interpose, "Well, what, after all, could such a little child create?" I reply, "This is what holy Scripture says." For instance, in Luke 2:11 we hear the dear angels sing at Christmas time, "To you is born this day in the city of David a Savior, who is Christ the Lord." That angelic song, in which Christ was called the Lord, was sung at a time when the Infant still clung to His mother's breast.

The fathers contended fervidly for this, maintaining against the heretics that there are two natures in Christ but not two persons, that there is only one Son. This is how Scripture speaks and how we, too, must speak. To be sure, Christ was crucified according to His humanity, and He created heaven and earth according to His divinity; but since this one person is God and man, it is proper to say that God's Son is the Creator of heaven and earth, and God's Son was also crucified. One dare not divide the person, leaving only the human nature; one must bear in mind that this person is also God. Thus Saint Hilary says, "When Christ suffered, the Logos was quiescent." If we fail to hold that the person who was crucified was both God and man, we are eternally damned and lost. We must have a Savior who is more than a saint or an angel. If He were not superior to these, we would get no help from Him. But if He is God, then the treasure is so heavy that it not only outweighs and cancels sin and death but also gives eternal life. No mere human could acquire eternal life for us or overcome devil and death.

This is our Christian creed, and in conformity with it we confess, "I believe in Jesus Christ, His only Son, our Lord, who was born of the Virgin Mary, suffered and died." Let heathen and heretics be ever so smart; hold firmly to this faith, and you will be saved. It follows, then, that whoever believes in the Son of man, who was born of Mary, who suffered and was buried, will not be lost but is a son of God in possession of eternal life. Devil, sin, and death will not be able to harm him, for he has eternal life.

Whosoever believes on Him will not perish but have everlasting life.

The text has good reason for adding that God gave His *only* Son and that believers in Him will not perish but have eternal life. For God has many other sons. We, for instance, glory in the fact that God is our Father, as we pray in the Our Father. And Saint Paul declares that God "destined us in love to be His sons through Jesus Christ" (Eph. 1:5). But the evangelist identifies these sons when he says, "These are sons who believe in the Son." It is logical that the Son in whom we believe must be distinct and different and greater than we, the sons of God who believe in Him. Others are also sons of God, but they are not such sons as is He in whom we must believe. He is not a Son of God by reason of His believing in us; we, however, become sons of God through our believing in Him. Therefore, His divine sonship is vastly different from yours or mine.

The heretics garbled holy Scripture terribly. They claimed that Christ is called a Son of God by a metaphor, as we, too, are called sons of God. In Job 38:4, 7 the angels are also termed sons of God. We read, "Where were you when the sons of God [that is, all the angels] worshiped Me in heaven?" They claim that Christ was a son of God in that sense too. But scrutinize this text. Here we learn that He is the Son in whom we must believe. We holy people and the angels are not sons of God such as He is; for we all become sons of God through our faith in Him. The angels, too, were made sons of God through Him; for they were all created by the Son, as we read in Colossians 1:16. We human beings were also created by Him, but we lost and condemned sinners become sons of God through our faith in Him. Christ, however, is God and the Son of God; for there is a great difference between the one who believes and the one in whom one believes. If someone deserves the honor that men believe in him and through that faith become children of God and achieve the new birth, such a person must be very God. Again, if He created the angels and if the angels take first rank among the creatures, then Christ must be Lord of all creatures. Likewise, since He created us men, He cannot be a son of God in the sense in which we or John the Baptist are sons of God.

This is the real difference between the other sons of God and this Son of God. He is God Himself, whereas we are made sons of God through Him; He gives us eternal life and through Himself overcomes death. These are essential differences. This is how you must interpret holy Scripture, not only for your own sake but also to enable you to cope with the schismatic spirits, who twist and interpret Scripture according to their own ideas. You must realize that this Son is holy, safe from devil and death, and is not subject to damnation as we humans are. Nor does He require salvation for Himself; for He has always been, and still is, salvation and life personified. He is very God not only in His person but also in

His office and His works. These bear witness to His divinity, as He says in John, "Even though you do not believe Me, believe Me for the sake of the works" (John 14:11). Therefore, it is a definition of His essence when this text says, "Whoever believes in Him has eternal life." It is He who bestows eternal life, kills death through Himself, and saves all who believe in Him. Such a work only God can do.

Your faith finds its vindication in the fact that Christ is very God in view not only of His essence and nature but also of His work. He is God in person, but He also performs the work of God: He saves those who believe in Him. Nowhere do we find it recorded that faith in any angel, whether Gabriel or Michael, or in John the Baptist or in the Virgin Mary, will make a person a child of God. Only of the Son is it said that He rescues from death and gives eternal life. Thus, Christ is established in the Godhead not only according to His person and majesty but also according to His work.

Therefore, it is fitting for us to write this text on every wall, and also in our hearts, with large, yes, with golden letters; for these are words of life and salvation. They teach us how to escape death and defend ourselves against all heretics, also against the pope and the Turk, all of whom read this text, but with drowsy eyes and deaf ears. For if they had heard, comprehended, and believed these words, they would not have fallen into such folly but would have said, "I am saved by Christ alone, who gave Himself into death for me." And if this is true, I am quick to add, "Well then, what am I doing in the cloister? Why did I run to Rome or to Saint James?" I did all this for the purpose of gaining salvation. And henceforth, I adjudge all religions and faiths false and heretical, whether of the Turk, of Mohammed, of the pope, or of the Jew, who also read and recite these words, but in the same indolent and indifferent manner in which the nuns read the Psalter without paying heed to its content. They, too, speak these words, but they only repeat them by rote like a parrot. But you must reflect on these words and impress them on your heart. And after you have gained a good understanding of them, you are in a position to examine and judge faith and to stand your ground against the attacks of the schismatic spirits.

Christ says further, "Ponder this, dear Nicodemus: that God so loved the world that He gave His only Son, that [you] should be saved by Him." As if He were to say, "I Myself perform the work of redemption from sin and death." And this work performed by Him, He gives or transfers to the Father, so that the Father's work and the Son's work are one and the same. The evangelist John consistently distinguishes between the persons, but he identifies the work. For the Father is not the son of the Virgin Mary, nor was He crucified, but only the Son; and yet Father and Son remain true God, and the Son draws us to the Father through Himself.

We heard Christ say, "That which is born of the flesh is flesh, and that which is born of the Spirit is spirit" (John 3:6); and, "No one has ascended into heaven but He who descended from heaven" (John 3:13). This is a hard and terrifying speech; it reflects nothing but the wrath of God. It condemns the whole world, deprives it of God, and leaves it lost and condemned. Yes, God is a real tyrant. You have heard of God's anger and judgment; you have heard that we all were conceived and born in sin. But now hear of the love of God, that He looks with favor on you and loves you. If you wish to have a gracious God and Father and know of His love for you, you must realize that you come to God by believing in the Son, whom the Father gave for you and who had Himself crucified for you. If this is your faith, it will be impossible for you not to feel the ineffable love of God manifested when He saved you from eternal doom and gave His Son that you might live. Hold firmly to this if you wish to be saved. For if you believe this, you ascend to heaven through Christ. Then you will not confront an angry judge but a dear Father, who is so kindly disposed toward you that He gave His Son for you; otherwise you would be lost. Now I can confidently say, "If God loved me so that He gave His only Son for my salvation, why should I fear His anger?"

In the papacy many sermons dealt with sin, death, and hell, and also with the wrath of God. But what did they say about deliverance from all this? They insisted that we render satisfaction for our sins with our good works and atone for them with monastic life, pilgrimages, and masses. But here we read, "Whoever does not believe in the Son has the wrath of God abiding over him." The pope, on the other hand, demands that I wear a cowl, be tonsured, and perform other tomfoolery to appease God's wrath. The Turk, the pope, and the Jews depict God as an angry God, but as one whose anger can be allayed and whose favor can be won if I humble myself, fast, sacrifice, perform good works, and expiate my sins with an ascetic life. It is the devil himself who directs people to their good works and not to Christ, the Son of God. God forbids us to rely on ourselves and boast of our good works, no matter how good they may be; and He insists that we approach the Son, take hold of Him, cleave to Him, believe in Him, and say, "I believe in Jesus Christ, the only Son of God, who was born of the Virgin Mary, who suffered and died for me."

The papists sang this in their churches daily, and they

also taught this creed to their children. However, no one understood it; otherwise no one would have said, "I want to escape hell with my monkery and my order." The Lord demands here that we refrain from all thoughts of finding God and attaining salvation by means of good works and seek refuge solely in Christ the Lord. For to seek God outside Christ leads to eternal damnation. Much could still be said on this subject if time permitted. At all times there have been many schismatic spirits who ignored Christ and wanted to climb up into heaven and seek God with their clever thoughts and their good works. All the heresies that were rampant among the Jews can be traced back to the hermits or Levites, who erected altars in their gardens, in beautiful fields, in bright meadows, under a pretty linden tree, or on a hill, whither they lured the people. Occasionally the devil would lend a hand with a miracle, and thus the people were miserably seduced. The prophets earnestly warned against this practice and condemned this self-devised zeal and worship of God. But when the clerics declared that this or that was to be done in these places because it was pleasing to God, the devil supported the suggestion. And the people flocked there in droves and established their own worship of God, just as though God were in agreement with them. He, however, had made it known through Moses where He wanted to be worshiped—not in any attractive spot, under a beautiful tree, in a gay meadow or field, or on a mountain, but at the place where the Ark of the Covenant rested. Thus, God was to be found only in the temple in Jerusalem. But the schismatic spirits retorted, "Why should God not also be found on this mountain or on the spot where Abraham, Isaac, and Jacob worshiped? God can hear us here as well as in Jerusalem." This meant climbing to God with one's own zeal. We did the same thing. We were not content with God's plan, "No one ascends into heaven but He who descends from heaven," and, "To escape damnation and to attain eternal life, one must believe in the crucified Son." No, we replied, "You must assuredly perform good works, not only the good works prescribed in the Ten Commandments—oh, no, these do not suffice! You must also do the good works commanded by the pope, such as fasting, observing holidays, etc." And now these people mock us when we preach about faith. They say, "Faith? Nonsense! No, whoever joins this or that order is saved." This is the trouble. This means seeking God in our own arbitrary way and trying to climb into heaven on the self-invented ladder of our own ideas. We must be on our guard against that devil whose name is Enthusiasm.[3] People who follow him disparage the oral Word and declare, "The Spirit must do it!" All they ever talk about is the Spirit. Of course, Nicodemus might have received the Spirit in this way too, but he gives ear to the Word of truth preached to him here by Christ, "No one ascends into heaven." The Word must still be preached and read orally, and the burden of our message must be, "I believe in the only Son of God, who died for me." We must seal our faith with the confession that we know of no other God than Him of whom we read here, "Whoever believes in the Son of man has everlasting life." No other thoughts or works will achieve this for me; the only way and the true way to God is to believe in the Son. Therefore, God has also commanded us to preach this diligently. That is why He established the ministry of oral preaching, instituted the sacraments,

---

[3]Luther uses the word *enthusiasmus* as a Latin translation of the German *Schwermerey*, his favorite name for the left wing of the Reformation.

and commanded absolution. He wanted this message to remain alive among Christians that faith might be preserved in wakeful hearts, a faith which confesses, "I believe in the Son, who was given into death for me." The papists, to be sure, hear these words too; for they possess the Bible as we do. But they slumber and snore over them; they have eyes and do not see, ears and do not hear. They say, "Oh, if only I had done what Saint Augustine or Saint Francis commanded!" The laity call upon the Virgin Mary to intercede for them with her Son. During my twenty years in the cloister I was obsessed with the one thought of observing the rules of my order. We were so drowned in the stupor of our own good works that we did not see and understand these words. But if you want to find God, then inscribe these words in your heart. Don't sleep, but be vigilant. Learn and ponder these words diligently, "God so loved the world that He gave His only Son, that whoever believes in Him should not perish but have eternal life." Let him who can write, write these words. Furthermore, read them, discuss them, meditate and reflect on them in the morning and in the evening, whether awake or asleep! For the devil will sorely assail your faith in an effort to make you doubt that Christ is the Son of God and that your faith is pleasing to God. He will torture you with thoughts of predestination, with the wrath and the judgment of God. Then you must say, "I don't want to hear or know anything else about God than that He loves me. I don't want to know anything about a wrathful God, about His judgment and anger, about hell, about death, and about damnation. But if I do see God's wrath, I know that this drives me to the Son, where I find refuge; and if I come to the Son, I also have a merciful Father." For Saint John tells us in his epistle that the Father loved me before I ever loved Him or knew Him, that He remitted my sin and gave me salvation (1 John 4:10).

Hearing these words and believing them makes a person a true Christian. But if one loses these words, all is lost, be you a Carthusian or whatever you will.

The words "not perish" are inexpressibly glorious. They mean to be rid of sin, to have a good conscience, and not to be under the law. Otherwise the law punishes sin; but now, even if someone feels sin and the wrath of God, sin will not give him a bad conscience, because his sin is forgiven. The law will not accuse him, sin will not bite or plague him, death will not devour him; for if he believes these words, he is safe and secure.

This is what we preach and believe. And let anyone who does not share this faith pray God that it may be imparted also to him. But see to it that you do not resist this faith or violate and blaspheme it, as the pope does when he says, "Of course, I know that Christ saves; but He does not save me." Well, the devil, too, knew that Christ saved Peter. Faith is not a paltry and petty matter as the pope's contempt of it would make it appear; but it is a heartfelt confidence in God through Christ that Christ's suffering and death pertain to you and should belong to you. The pope and the devil have a faith too, but it is only a "historical faith." True faith does not doubt; it yields its whole heart to the conviction that the Son of God was given into death for us, that sin is remitted, that death is destroyed, and that these evils have been done away with—but, more than this, that eternal life, salvation, and glory, yes, God Himself have been restored to us, and that through the Son God has made us His children.

These are living words which Christ addresses to us, to you and to me, when He says that he who accepts the

Son shall be saved and that death, devil, and hell shall be disposed of for him. These words comfort us when we are frightened and troubled or when we contend against the schismatic spirits. They extinguish the flaming darts of the devil (Eph. 6:16). They assure us that we retain the glory that God's Son is our gift and our treasure. This conviction cannot be imparted to us by any monastic order or rule, whether it be named for Saint Augustine or anyone else. No, you must say, "I believe in Christ, in whom Saint Augustine also believed." But if I were to say, "Oh, you dear Virgin Mary, you are holier than I. And you, Saint Francis, have many merits; transfer some of them to my credit!" it would all be vain. The same answer would be given to you that, according to Matthew 25:9, was given to the five foolish virgins when they wished to borrow from the wise virgins, who had their lamps full of oil: "Go to the dealers and buy for yourselves"; that is, go to your preachers and teachers, who misinformed you so.

Thus, we find rich, excellent, and salutary words in this text. They should be diligently heeded.

The theme of Romans 5 is justification by faith. This concept was the key to Luther's own awakening, and he expounded this message with great fervor during the Reformation.

Luther witnessed the Catholic church's sale of indulgences, as people paid the church for the hope of gaining eternal life. As he teaches, Romans 5 makes it clear that the gospel is not for sale, nor is it limited to a particular group. Salvation is a free gift of God made available to all who believe.

Luther's exposition is thorough and practical. He deals directly with important theological issues such as God's wrath and love, and Christ's death and resurrection. The impact of this message is a crucial factor in understanding the gospel.

CHAPTER SIX

Romans 5

**Therefore since we are justified by faith,
we have peace with God.**

This is the spiritual peace of which all the
prophets sing. And because this is the case, he adds the
words *with God*. And this peace is prefigured in every
peace which the children of Israel enjoyed in days of old.

And this is the real peace of conscience and trust in
God. Just as on the contrary a spiritual disturbance is
the lack of a quiet conscience and a mistrust of God.
Thus Hosea says, "For they sow the wind, and they shall
reap the whirlwind" (Hos. 8:7). For the penalty of a bad
conscience is stated in Psalm 1:4 to be "like the chaff
which the wind drives away."

Thus Christ is also called the Prince of Peace and a
Solomon (cf. Isa. 9:6; 1 Chr. 22:9). Ephesians 2:14, 17
reads, "He is our peace, who has made us both one. . . .

And He came and preached peace to you who were far off and peace to those who were near." The same idea is expressed in Isaiah 57:19, and in John 16:33, "That in Me you may have peace; in the world you have tribulation." The other kind of peace is carnal, of which He says, "I have not come to bring peace, but a sword" (Matt. 10:34). By contrast there is the carnal disturbance and temporal quietness. Hence also Psalm 72:7, "In His days shall righteousness flourish, and peace abound," must not be understood in the sense of the temporal peace which existed under Augustus, as many think, but of this spiritual peace "with God."

But note how the apostle places this spiritual peace only after righteousness has preceded it. For first he says, "since we are justified by faith," and then, "we have peace." Thus also in Psalm 85:10, "Righteousness and peace have kissed," the term "righteousness" precedes the word "peace." And again, "In His days shall righteousness flourish, and peace abound" (Ps. 72:7). And here the perversity of men seeks peace before righteousness, and for this reason they do not find peace. Thus the apostle creates a very fine antithesis in these words, namely,

The righteous man has peace with God but affliction in the world, because he lives in the Spirit.

The unrighteous man has peace with the world but affliction and tribulation with God, because he lives in the flesh.

But as the Spirit is eternal, so also will be the peace of the righteous man and the tribulation of the unrighteous.

And as the flesh is temporal, so will be the tribulation of the righteous and the peace of the unrighteous.

Hence we read in Isaiah 57:21 and 48:22, "There is no peace for the wicked, says the Lord," that is, spiritually, for there surely is a peace for the wicked; in Psalm 73:3, "For I was envious of the arrogant when I saw the prosperity of the wicked"; and in Psalm 28:3, "Who speak peace with their neighbor while mischief (that is, not peace, but disturbance and restlessness toward God) is in their hearts."

Through whom we have obtained access by faith.

In a most useful manner the apostle joins together these two expressions, "through Christ" and "by faith," as he did also above in the expression "since we are justified by faith . . . through our Lord." In the first place, the statement is directed against those who are so presumptuous as to believe that they can approach God without Christ, as if it were sufficient for them to have believed by faith alone, not through Christ, but beside Christ, as if after accepting the grace of justification they no longer needed Him. And now there are many people who from the works of faith make for themselves works of the law and of the letter, when having received faith by baptism and penitence, they now think that they are personally pleasing to God even without Christ, when actually both are necessary, namely, to have faith and also always to possess Christ as our mediator in this faith. Hence we read in Psalm 91:1, "He who dwells in the shelter of the Most High shall abide in the shadow of God in heaven." Faith makes the dwelling place, but Christ the protection and the aid. And later we read, "He will cover you with His [feathers], and under His wings you will trust" (Ps. 91:4); and in Malachi 4:2, "But for you who fear My name the Sun of righteousness shall rise with healing in His wings"; and in Psalm 31:2, "Be Thou unto me a God, a protector and a house of refuge"; and again in Psalm 90:1, "Lord, Thou hast been our dwelling place." Thus, the apostle is interpreting these and all similar authoritative expressions of Scripture, together with many other figurative expressions of the law.

But in our day the hypocrites and legalists swell up with horrifying pride and think that they are now saved and sufficiently righteous because they believe in Christ, but they are unwilling to be considered unrighteous or regarded as fools. And what is this except the rejection of Christ's protection and a desire to approach God only from faith but not through Christ? Indeed, then there is not faith at all, but only the appearance. So at sunset the rays of the sun and the light of the sun go down together. But he who is wise does not set such high value on the light that he no longer needs the sun, rather he wants to have both the sun and the light at the same time. Therefore, those who approach God through faith and not at the same time through Christ actually depart from Him.

Second, the apostle is speaking against those who rely too heavily on Christ and not enough on faith, as if they were to be saved through Christ in such a way that they themselves had to do nothing and show no evidence of faith. These people have too much faith, or actually none at all. For this reason it is necessary to emphasize both points: "through faith" and "through Christ," so that we do and suffer everything which we possibly can in faith in Christ. And yet in all of these activities we must confess that we are unprofitable servants, believing that only through Christ are we made worthy to approach God.

For in all works of faith we must strive to make ourselves worthy of Christ and His righteousness as our protection and refuge. "Therefore, since we are justified by faith" and our sins are forgiven, "we have access and peace," but only "through our Lord Jesus Christ." This also applies to those who follow the mystical theology and struggle in inner darkness, omitting all pictures of Christ's suffering, wishing to hear and contemplate only the uncreated Word Himself, but not having first been justified and purged in the eyes of their heart through the incarnate Word. For the incarnate Word is first necessary for the purity of the heart, and only when one has this purity, can he through this Word be taken up spiritually into the uncreated Word. But who is there who thinks that he is so pure that he dares aspire to this level unless he is called and led into the rapture by God, as was the case with the apostle Paul, or unless he is "taken up with Peter, James, and John, his brother" (Matt. 17:1)? In brief, this rapture is not called an "access."

We rejoice in our sufferings.

From this text we clearly see the distinction of a twofold wrath and a twofold mercy of God and also of a twofold suffering. For there is a kind of suffering that comes from His severity and another from His kindness. That suffering which comes from His kindness, because of its nature, works only things which are very good, although by an accident something different may take place. But this is not His fault but the fault of him to whom it happens because of his weakness; for he does not know the true nature of his suffering and its power and working. He judges and esteems it according to its outward appearance, that is, in a wrong way, since it ought to be adored as the very cross of Christ.

Of whatever quality suffering finds characteristics

and people to be, it makes them even more [so]. Thus if a person is carnal, weak, blind, evil, irascible, arrogant, when trial comes, he becomes more carnal, weaker, blinder, more evil, more irascible, more arrogant. And on the other hand, if he is spiritual, brave, wise, good, meek, and humble, he becomes more spiritual, braver, wiser, better, meeker, and humbler. In Psalm 4:1 we read, "Thou hast given me room when I was in distress." But concerning the other kind of people, Matthew 7:27 says, "The floods came and the winds blew and beat against that house, and great was the fall thereof."

Those people talk nonsense who attribute their bad temper or their impatience to that which causes them offense or suffering. For suffering does not make a person impatient but merely shows that he has been or is still impatient. Thus, a person learns in suffering what kind of man he is, just as the glutton does when he itches.

Rude, puerile, and even hypocritical are those people who venerate the relics of the holy cross with the highest outward honor and then flee from and curse their sufferings and adversities. This is obvious, for in Scripture tribulations are expressly called the cross of Christ, as in 1 Corinthians 1:17, "Lest the cross of Christ be emptied of its power"; "And he who does not take his cross and follow Me" (Matt. 10:38); and, "Why am I still persecuted? In that case the stumbling block of the cross has been removed" (Gal. 5:11); and, "I tell you with tears that they live as enemies of the cross of Christ" (Phil. 3:18). But our theologians and priests today think of nothing else in the term "enemies of the cross of Christ" but Turks and Jews, as the theologians of Cologne did against John Reuchlin, and as the papal bulls and the glosses of the lawyers do.

But they themselves are actually "the enemies of the cross of Christ." For it is true that only the friends of the cross are its enemies, according to the statement in Psalm 38:11, "My friends and companions have stood against Me." "And they who praised Me swore against Me" (Ps. 102:8). For who hates tribulation and suffering more than the priests and the lawyers? Indeed, who seeks riches, pleasures, leisure, honors, and glories more than they do?

Whoever is unwilling to suffer tribulation should never think that he is a Christian, but rather a Turk and an enemy of Christ. For here he is speaking about all of us when he says: "We rejoice in our sufferings." In Acts 14:22 we read, "Through many tribulations we must . . ." "We must," he says, not "it just happens" or "it may be the case" or "we are disposed to." And in 1 Peter 1:6 we read, "Though now for a little while you may have to suffer various trials." "Have to," he says, that is, it absolutely cannot take place in any other way.

But we must note this: there are two kinds of enemies of the cross of Christ. The first kind is the violent type, and the second is the cunning. The violent are those who want to make the cross of no effect by force, and they attack it with all their forces; they are the ones who seek vengeance against anyone who offends them, and they are neither willing nor able to be at rest until they have been vindicated. They fall into many evils, such as hatred, detractions, abuses, rejoicing at the evils which befall their neighbor and sorrow over his good fortune.

But the cunning enemies are those who desert the cross in flight, that is, those who do not want to speak or perform the truth for anyone but are always trying to please, to wheedle, to flatter everyone and to offend no one, or else they withdraw into solitude (at least for this reason). The apostle refers to such people in Galatians 6:12, when he says, "It is those who want to make a good showing in the flesh that would compel you to be circumcised, and only that they may not be persecuted for the cross of Christ."

We must note that this climax or gradation is also contrary to those who do not stand in this grace, namely, that suffering works impatience, and impatience rejection, and rejection despair, and despair eternal confounding. And thus finally the hatred of God will be poured out (that is, it will be recognized that it has been poured out whenever this hatred reaches its completion) in their hearts through the wicked spirit under whose dominion they have been delivered. Therefore I said that the impatient man is not yet a Christian, at least before God, because he is found to have been rejected through suffering.

Hence, since the Lord in many passages is given the name of Savior and Helper in suffering, he who is unwilling to suffer as much as he can deprives Him of His true titles and names. Thus to this man there will be no Jesus, that is, no Savior, because he is unwilling to be damned; for him there will be no God the Creator because he is unwilling to be nothing, so that He may be his Creator. God will be no power, wisdom, or good to him, because he does not want Him to uphold him in his weakness, his foolishness, or his punishment.

Endurance and trial.

The different degrees of impatience are known from the degrees of anger which the Lord shows in Matthew 5:21–22, when He is explaining the commandment "You shall not kill." For because impatience is the cause of anger, the effect of both is the same, unless someone should separate impatience from anger. Then its degrees are more intensive than extensive. For an impatient man is patient in nothing. But the apostle here clearly indicates the degrees of endurance. Baptista Mantuanus distinguishes very carefully among these degrees. The lowest is to bear sufferings only with difficulty and with a mind which prefers to be delivered from the trial. The second and medium degree is to bear it with joy to be sure and willingly, but not to seek it. The highest degree is to long for suffering, to seek it like a treasure and to bring it about. This is the meaning of the words "we rejoice in our sufferings" and also of the statement in Galatians 6:14, "We must glory in the cross of our Lord."

The expression "trial" in this passage must be understood in a good sense, namely, as the goal of suffering, as that which is sought through tribulation. For God accepts no one as righteous whom He has not first tested, and He proves him through no other means than through the fire of tribulation, as we read in Psalm 17:3, "Thou hast tried me by fire, and iniquity has not been found in me." And there is this statement of Ecclesiasticus 44:16–17, "He pleased God, . . . and he was found perfect"; and again, ". . . he who is found without blemish" (Ecclesiasticus 31:8); also, "The Lord tests the righteous and the wicked" (Ps. 11:5). Thus one comes to this testing in no other way than through endurance. And this testing takes place in order that each person may see his own state of mind, that is, that each may know himself, whether he really loves God for the sake of God, which God of course knows even without any testing. Thus we read, "Search me, O God, and know my heart" (that is, make it known also to me). "Try me and know my paths. And see if there be any wicked way in me, and lead me in the way everlasting" (Ps. 139:23–24). This passage very beautifully expresses the reason why God brings tribulations to men, in order that He might test them, that is, make them approved through endurance. For if God should not test us by tribulation, it would be impossible for any man to be saved.

The reason is that our nature has been so deeply curved in upon itself because of the viciousness of original sin that it not only turns the finest gifts of God in upon itself and enjoys them (as is evident in the case of legalists and hypocrites), indeed, it even uses God Himself to achieve these aims. It also seems to be ignorant of this very fact, that in acting so iniquitously, so perversely, and in such a depraved way, it is even seeking God for its own sake. Thus the prophet Jeremiah says, "The heart is perverse above all things, and desperately corrupt; who can understand it?" (Jer. 17:9); that is, it is so curved in on itself that no man, no matter how holy (if a testing is kept from him) can understand it. Thus Psalm 19:12 reads: "Who can discern his errors? Clear Thou me from hidden faults," and, "Therefore, let everyone who is godly offer prayer to Thee at a proper time." (Ps. 32:6). And the Scripture calls this viciousness by a name most proper to it, that is, iniquity, depravity, or crookedness. The doctor of *The Sentences*[1] deals with this subject in a discussion of enjoyment and use and of the love of friendship and the love of concupiscence. Therefore, if we have said that iniquity is this very impatience, or at least the cause of this impatience, then this crookedness is also iniquity, which of necessity is hostile to the cross. The cross puts to death everything we have,

---

[1]This is a reference to the great medieval theologian, Peter the Lombard. His classic work *The Sentences* became the required theological text in the major medieval universities.

but our iniquity tries to keep itself and its possessions alive. Therefore, our good God, after He has justified us and given us His spiritual gifts, quickly brings tribulation upon us, exercises us, and tests us so that this godless nature of ours does not rush in upon these enjoyable sins, lest in his ignorance man should die the eternal death. For they are very lovely and vigorously excite enjoyment. Thus man learns to love and worship God purely for Himself, and not just because of His grace and His gifts; but he worships God for His own sake alone. Thus, "He chastises every son whom He receives" (Heb. 12:6). And unless He did this, the son would quickly be drawn away by the sweetness of his new inheritance, he would luxuriate in his enjoyment of the grace which he had received and would offend his Father more deeply than before. Therefore, in very good order the apostle says, "Suffering produces endurance, and endurance trial," that is, a proving or a testing.

And hope does not disappoint us.

Without a testing of this sort, as I have said, hope would founder, indeed, it would no longer be hope, but presumptuousness; in fact, it would be worse, for it would be the enjoyment of the creature instead of the Creator. And if a person remained in this state, he would be confounded for all eternity. Therefore, suffering comes, through which a man is made patient and tested; it comes and takes away everything he has and leaves him naked and alone, allowing him no help or safety in either his physical or spiritual merits. It makes a man despair of all created things, to turn away from them and from himself, to seek help outside of himself and all other things, in God alone, and thus to sing in the words of Psalm 3:3, "But Thou, O Lord, art my Protector and my Glory." This is what it means to hope, and that hope is created in times of testing, while of necessity the ungodly, who are accustomed to trust in their own powers, are unwilling to remain calm and to endure their tribulations in order that they may be tested. In the final test, since they do not know how to trust solely in God, after their substance has been ruined and the mountains of their own achievements have fallen down, then they themselves fall into ruin for eternity. "Then they will begin to say to the mountains, 'Fall upon us'" (Luke 23:30; cf. Hos. 10:8). For their hope was not a real hope, but a perverse presumptuousness, a confidence in their own works and their own righteousness.

But yet we must know that suffering is of two kinds. The first is physical, in which men who are carnal are overcome; they fail because of their concern for physical goods, for things, for the body, for reputation, and they depart from God, lose hope because of their impatience, and thus deliver themselves up to the flesh and forsake God. Of such people the apostle says, "They have become callous and have given themselves up to licentiousness" (Eph. 4:19). The second is the suffering of conscience and spirit, wherein all of one's self-righteousness and wisdom in which people trust are devoured and done away. Of these the Savior says, in a mystical way, "When a strong man fully armed . . . but when one stronger than he assails him and overcomes him, he takes away his armor and binds him and divides his spoils" (Luke 11:21–22), that is, he will strip a man who is fortified with his own righteousnesses and will teach him that they are to be used for the common good and not for his own pleasure.

For God's love has been poured into our hearts through the Holy Spirit who has been given to us.

This expression ought to be understood as instruction in the Holy Spirit, as to why and how we can glory in our sufferings, namely, that we might learn that of ourselves and of our own powers it is impossible, but that it is a gift of the love which is given by the Holy Spirit.

Therefore, "God's love," which is the purest feeling toward God and alone makes us right at heart, alone takes away iniquity, alone extinguishes the enjoyment of our own righteousness. For it loves nothing but God alone, not even His gifts, as the hypocritical self-righteous people do. Therefore, when physical and spiritual blessings flow in, it does not get excited. Again, when they disappear, and physical and spiritual evils deluge us, it is not crushed. But "Knowledge puffs up" (1 Cor. 8:1), and so does righteousness. Again, ignorance humbles us, and so does sin. "But love bears all things" (1 Cor. 13:7), even glorying in its tribulations. Therefore, we must note that; it is called "God's love" because by it we love God alone, where nothing is visible, nothing experiential, either inwardly or outwardly, in which we can trust or which is to be loved or feared. It is carried away beyond all things into the invisible God, who cannot be experienced, who cannot be comprehended, that is, into the midst of the shadows, not knowing what it loves, only knowing what it does not love; turning away from everything which it has known and experienced, and desiring only that which it has not yet known, saying, "I am sick with love" (Song of Sol. 2:5), that is, I do not want what I have and I do not have what I want. But this gift is far removed from those who still look at their own righteousnesses, trust in them, feel secure in them, and thus do not "rejoice in sufferings," are not tested, and thus have no hope.

Thus the apostle asserts that this sublime power which is in us is not from ourselves, but must be sought from God. Thus it follows that it *is poured* into us, not born in us or originated in us. And this takes place *through the Holy Spirit;* it is not acquired by moral effort and practice, as our moral virtues are. *Into our hearts,* that is, into the depths and the midst and center of our hearts, not on the surface of the heart, as foam lies on water. This is the kind of love that the hypocrites have, who imagine and pretend that they have love. But a period of testing only proves the pride and impatience which lies deep within them.

Who has been given to us, that is, whom we do not deserve, rather we deserve the direct opposite. But he proves that this is true, because now follows, "He is really given" and not deserved. For Christ "died for the weak" (v. 6) and not for the strong and the deserving. Thus it is called *love* to indicate the difference between this and the unworthy and low kind of love by which a creature is loved; for the term "love" means to love something very dearly and preciously and to regard as very precious the thing that is loved. For this is what it means to love God above all things and to esteem Him with a rich love, that is, to love Him with a precious love. But to love Him for the sake of His gifts or for some advantage is the lowest kind of love, that is, to love Him with a selfish desire. This is using God but not enjoying Him.[2] *God's* love is used because only God is loved in this way,

---

[2]Luther is no doubt indebted to Augustine's discussion of the difference between "using" and "enjoying" in *De doctrina Christiana*, where Augustine compares the Christian pilgrim to a traveler far from home who "uses" a conveyance to return home but does not "enjoy" the journey for

not even the neighbor, except for the sake of God, that is, because God so wills, and one loves His will above all things.

We must also note that love dwells nowhere but in the heart, indeed, in the innermost center of the heart, and for this reason there is that difference between sons and bond servants. The sons serve Him happily, willingly, and freely, not in fear of punishment or desire for glory, but only to fulfill the will of God; but the bond servants are forced by the fear of punishment, and they serve Him unwillingly and with great difficulty, or they are desirous of a reward, in which case they serve Him willingly enough but with a mercenary intent, but never absolutely out of a desire to fulfill His will. Particularly in time of tribulation does the servant and the hireling run away, but the son perseveres, as John 10:12 says: "But the hireling flees." Thus He says to them, "Oh, that there were one among you who would shut the doors, that you might not kindle fire on my altar in vain!" (Mal. 1:10). And then He continues, "I have no pleasure in you, says the Lord of Hosts," for they are actually very presumptuous and believe that they are carrying out the will of God. This is the reason why in the same place, when the Lord has said, "You offer polluted bread upon My altar," they reply as if they could not imagine this to be possible, saying, "How have we polluted it?" (Mal. 1:7–8) which is to say, "In our opinion we have done everything which Thou has commanded." The Lord replies, "When you offer blind animals for sacrifice, is that no evil? And when you offer those that are lame or sick, is that no

---

its own sake. In the same way, says Augustine, "if we wish to return to our Father's home, this world must be used, not enjoyed. . . . The true objects of enjoyment are the Father and the Son and the Holy Spirit, who are at the same time the Trinity, one Being."

evil?" That is, they worship God without true love but with a desire for their own advantage, like hirelings, not having the single eye of the bride, with which she sees only the invisible God and nothing of her own things or those of any other creature.

Note again how the apostle unites the spring with the river. He speaks of the "love . . . through the Holy Spirit, who is given to us." For it is not enough to have the gift unless the giver also be present, as Moses also begged in Exodus 33:15, "If Thy presence will not go with me, do not carry us up from here." Indeed, properly it is to love alone that the apostle attributes the presence and at the same time the giving of the Spirit. For all other gifts, as he says in 1 Corinthians 12:7 ff, are given by the same Spirit but are not the Spirit Himself. Just so he says here regarding love that it is not given unless the Spirit Himself has first been given, who then spreads this love abroad in our hearts. But in that passage he says, "But all these gifts are inspired by one and the same Spirit" (v. 11). Hence he goes on to say in the same chapter, "I will show you a still more excellent way" (v. 31). Or at least, even if He is given in all the gifts, yet He does not pour forth love in all.

At the right time.

Some refer this expression to the statement which follows, so that the meaning is "When we were still weak, He died for the ungodly according to time," as if to say that, although He is eternal and immortal, yet He died in time. He died because of His humanity which lived in time, but He is alive forever because of His deity, which lives in eternity. Others interpret it thus, "He died at the time when we were weak," that is, He died at the time when we were not yet righteous and whole, but rather weak and sickly, so that the meaning is, "at the right time," namely, at that time when we were still weak. And this interpretation is the better one, as becomes evident in what follows: *For if, while we were enemies we were reconciled to God by the death of His Son* (v. 10). But others refer the expression to the preceding sentence, so that the meaning is when we were weak according to time, even though before God we were already righteous through His predestination. For in the predestination of God all things have already taken place, even things which in our reality still lie in the future.

Therefore, as sin through one man.

That the apostle is in this passage talking about original sin and not actual sin is proved in many passages, and we assume this to be so from these points:

First, because he says, "through one man." Thus Augustine says in his work *On the Merits of Sins and Their Remission,* "If the apostle had wanted to point out that sin came into this world not by propagation but by imitation, he would not have spoken of Adam as the one who originated it, but rather of the devil, . . . of whom it is said in Wisdom of Solomon 2:24, 'And they follow him who are of his side.' " In this sense Adam also imitated him and thus had the devil as the originating cause of his sin. But here the apostle says, "through a man." All actual sins enter and have entered the world through the devil, but original sin came through this one man. Blessed Augustine also says, "Thus, when the apostle mentions that sin and the death which passed from this one man to all men through propagation, he makes him the originating cause from whom the propagation of the human race took its beginning." Chrysostom says regarding this passage, "It is clear that it is not the sin which comes from the transgression of the law but the sin which derives from the disobedience of Adam, which contaminates all things."

Second, he says, "Through one man," because actual sin is committed by many, since every man brings his own sin into the world.

Third, he says, "Sin came into the world." But no actual sin enters the world, for each man's sin hangs over him, as we read in Ezekiel 18:20, that each will carry his own sin. Therefore, it does not come upon others but remains on each person individually. And that the term "world" does not mean heaven and earth in this passage but only the men in the world is clear from Romans 3:6, "How could God judge the world?" and 1 John 5:19, "The whole world is in the power of the evil one." In John 3:16 we read, "God so loved the world"; and later on, "If the world hates you . . ." (John 15:18); again, "I chose you out of the world" (John 15:19). And the reason is that the physical world is insensitive and incapable of sinning, so that sin and death could not enter it. For it neither dies nor sins, but man both sins and dies; therefore, for sin to enter the world means that the world becomes guilty and sinful because of one man. As we read below, "As by one man's disobedience many were made sinners" (v. 19).

Fourth, *death through sin,* because it is certain that the death of the world (that is, of all men) does not come from the personal sin of each man, since even those who have not sinned die. Therefore, if death comes by sin and if without sin there would be no death, then sin is in all of us. Thus it is not personal sin that he is talking about here. Otherwise it would be false to say that death had entered by sin, but rather we ought to say that it came by the will of God.

Fifth, because he says *death spread to all men,* even if death came because of our personal sin, yet it comes upon only him who commits it, as the Law says : "The fathers shall not be put to death for the children" (Deut. 24:16).

Sixth, he uses the term "sin " in the singular, referring to one. But if he had wanted us to understand this passage of actual sin, he would use the plural, as he does below, when he speaks of "many trespasses" (v. 16), where he is clearly comparing that one particular sin with many others, and from this he concludes that the efficacy of grace is greater than that of sin.

Seventh, *in which all men sinned.* There is nothing else "in which all men sinned," but each sins his own.

Eighth, *sin was in the world before the Law was given,* (v. 13). Actual sin also was in the world before Moses, and it was imputed, because it was also punished by men; but original sin was unknown until Moses revealed it in Genesis 3.

Ninth, he says here that their *sins were not like the transgressions of Adam* (v. 14), that is, an exact simulation of his sin but nevertheless they all sin with actual sin who commit sin.

Tenth, *Adam is a type of the One who was to come,* but not by actual sin; for otherwise all men would be a figure of Christ, but now only Adam is that figure, because of the extension of his one sin to all men.

But now in order to confound and overturn the perversity of future heretics, whom he foresaw in spirit, the apostle in explaining how Adam is the figure of Christ speaks only in the singular, for fear that some impudent sophist might reduce it to nonsense by saying: "He is taking the word 'sin' in a collective sense, using it in the singular rather than the plural, as the Scripture frequently does." Thus he says expressly, "through one man who sinned" (v. 12), and, "the effect of that one man's sin unto condemnation" (v. 16), and again, "because of one man's trespass" (v. 17), again, "by one man's trespass" (v. 18), and "by one man's disobedience" (v. 19). This point of comparison is particularly strong, "For the judgment following one trespass brought condemnation, but the free gift following many trespasses brings justification" (v. 16). For "judgment (as blessed Augustine says) leads from many offenses unto justification." But since he does not say this, however, but rather "by one," it is easy to see that he is speaking of original sin. Likewise, he denies that many sinned, but only the one, when he says "through one man's trespass" (v. 15) and "one man's sin" (v. 18) and "one man's sin" (v. 16). Note how at the same time it is true that only one man sinned, that only one sin was committed, that only one person was disobedient, and yet because of him many were made sinners and disobedient.

What, therefore, is original sin?

First, according to the subtle distinctions of the scholastic theologians, original sin is the privation or lack of original righteousness. And righteousness, according to these men, is only something subjective in the will, and therefore also the lack of it, its opposite. This comes under the category of a quality, according to the *Logic* and *Metaphysics* of Aristotle.

Second, however, according to the apostle and the simplicity of meaning in Christ Jesus, it is not only a lack of a certain quality in the will, nor even only a lack of light in the mind or of power in the memory, but particularly it is a total lack of uprightness and of the power of all the faculties both of body and soul and of the whole inner and outer man. On top of all this, it is a propensity toward evil. It is a nausea toward the good, a loathing of light and wisdom, and a delight in error and darkness, a flight from and an abomination of all good works, a pursuit of evil, as it is written in Psalm 14:3, "They are all gone astray, they are all alike corrupt"; and, "For the imagination and thought of man's heart are evil from his youth" (Gen. 8:21). For God hates and imputes not only this lack (even as many forget their own sin and no longer acknowledge it) but also this universal concupiscence by which we become disobedient to the commandment "You shall not covet" (Exod. 20:17; Deut. 5:21). As the apostle most clearly argues later on in chapter 7, this commandment shows us our sin: "I should not have known what it is to covet if the Law had not said, 'You shall not covet.'"

Therefore, as the ancient holy fathers[3] so correctly said, this original sin is the very tinder of sin, the law of the flesh, the law of the members, the weakness of our nature, the tyrant, the original sickness. For it is like a sick man whose mortal illness is not only the loss of health of one of his members, but it is, in addition to the lack of health in all his members, the weakness of all of his senses and powers, culminating even in his disdain

---

[3]The formulation is mainly that of Peter Lombard, but this is heavily dependent on Augustine. For Luther ancient fathers often means Augustine.

for those things which are healthful and in his desire for those things which make him sick. Thus, this is Hydra,[4] a many-headed and most tenacious monster, with which we struggle in the Lernean Swamp of this life till the very day of our death. It is Cerberus,[5] that irrepressible barker, and Antaeus,[6] who cannot be overcome while loose here on the earth. I have not found so clear a discussion of the subject of original sin as in Gerard Groote's treatise *Blessed Is the Man*,[7] in which he speaks not as an arrogant philosopher but as a sound theologian.

Therefore, to think that original sin is merely the lack of righteousness in the will is merely to give occasion for lukewarmness and a breakdown of the whole concept of penitence, indeed, to implant pride and presumptuousness, to eradicate the fear of God, to outlaw humility, to make the command of God invalid, and thus condemn it completely. At least, this is the situation if these theologians are taken at their word! And as a result, one can easily become proud over against another man, when he thinks that he himself is free from a sin in which he sees his neighbor still struggling.

This is why many people, in order that they may have a

---

[4]In Greek mythology a monster that inhabited the swamps of Lerna in the Peloponnesus. When one of its nine heads was cut off, it was immediately replaced by two new ones, unless cauterized. Hercules slew this dragon.

[5]The surly, three-headed dog that guarded the gates to Hades. In his most difficult "twelfth labor" Hercules subdued this formidable beast. Cf. Vergil, *Aeneid*, VI, 698.

[6]The giant whose strength was constantly renewed so long as he remained in contact with his mother, Earth. Hercules crushed him while holding him aloft.

[7]Gerard Groote wrote no such tract. Luther must be thinking of Gerard Zerbolt of Zütphen, whose tract *De spiritualibus ascensionibus* begins with these words of Ps. 84:6.

reason for humility, busy themselves with exaggerating their past sins and those that they possibly could have committed, and they do the same thing regarding their present sins, so that they may appear humble because of their attention to them. Here is good instruction. But there obviously are also present sins, and they permit no hint of superiority or complacency to gain the upper hand in us at the condemnation of someone else (which often is the case). For the real reason for humility is obvious, namely, that sin remains in us, but "it has no dominion over us" (Rom. 6:14), but it is subject to the Spirit, so that a person may destroy what formerly ruled over him. Therefore, if anyone looks down on another man as a sinner, sin still rules him doubly. For since he himself is a sinner, he compares himself as a righteous man to the other person and thus makes himself a liar and does not realize as a sinner that he is a sinner. Properly speaking, this is iniquity. For it is prohibited to judge, and yet he judges. But a man cannot judge unless he is superior and better. Therefore in this very act he is proudly preferring himself to the other, and in this way he sins, although he has committed no other sin than that he has forgotten that he himself is a sinner and that he has considered himself to be righteous. Therefore, whoever realizes that sin is in him, which he must govern, this man will surely fear to become a servant of sin, especially will he be afraid of judging. For if he judges, he knows that the Lord will say to him, Why do you judge like a righteous man, when you are unrighteous? And even if you have been righteous, yet because you trust in your own righteousness, you have already polluted it and have created a twofold unrighteousness, since you set up your sin as righteousness and then boast of it as righteousness."

Sin came into the world. The apostle uses this particular expression to indicate that original sin does not come from men but rather that it comes to them. For it is the nature of actual sin that it comes out of us, as the Lord says, "For out of the heart come evil thoughts" (Matt. 15:19). But this sin enters into men, and they do not commit it but suffer it, as Moses says, "And there came out this calf" (Exod. 32:24).

In which all have sinned. This is unclear in the Greek as to whether it is masculine or neuter. Thus it seems that the apostle wants it understood in both senses. Hence blessed Augustine also interprets it in both ways . . . saying, " 'in that all have sinned.' It surely is clear and obvious that personal sins, in which only those who have committed them are involved, are one thing and that this one sin in which all have taken part insofar as all were in this one man is something quite different." From this statement of Augustine it would seem to follow that original sin is the very first sin, namely, the transgression of Adam. For he interprets the expression "all men sinned" with reference to a work which has actually been committed and not only with reference to the transmission of guilt. He continues, "But if that one man and not sin is referred to, in that all have sinned in this one man, what can be clearer than this clear expression?" But the first interpretation is better in view of what follows. For later on the apostle says, "For as by one man's disobedience many were made sinners" (v. 19), and this is the same as saying that all have sinned in the sin of the one man. But even so the second interpretation can be advanced, that is, while one man sinned, all men sinned. Thus, in Isaiah 43:26 f., "Set forth your case, that you may be proved right. Your first father sinned," which is to say, you cannot be justified, because you are the son of Adam, who sinned first.

Therefore, you also are a sinner, because you are the son of a sinner; but a sinner can beget nothing but another sinner like himself.

Sin indeed was in the world before the Law was given.

In regard to this verse Augustine has this to say, "This means that the law, either natural or written, could not take away sin. For by the works of the law no one can be justified." And elsewhere, in his *Exposition of Certain Propositions*, he says, "The expression 'before the law was given, sin was in the world' must be understood in the sense 'until grace should come.' For he is speaking against those who think that sin can be taken away by the law. And he says that sins are made manifest by the law but are not taken away, since the Scripture says, 'Sin was not counted where there was no law.' For it does not say that sin did not exist but that it was not imputed. Nor was sin taken away when the law was given; rather it began to be imputed, that is, to be made manifest. Therefore, we should not think that the expressions 'before the law' is to be understood as if there were no sin under the law, for the term 'before the law' is spoken in the sense that he counts the entire time of the law until the end of the law, which is Christ."

And in this way blessed Augustine ties the expression "before the law" to the expression "sin was in the world." But then it becomes necessary to say, as he himself does say, that sin was not only until the law, but much more so under the law, which entered that the offense might abound. But if one takes the expression in connection with the negative phrase "sin was not counted," then it is not necessary to take such a harsh interpretation of the phrase "before the law," which in any case indicates the end. The meaning then is [that] before the law, sin (which, however, was always in the world) was not imputed, which is to say, it was not counted or known until the law came, which brought it forth, not in actual being, for it already was in existence, but in the sense that it became known. Or thus, "Before the law, sin was in the world," that is, it was merely there, only insofar as it existed, but beyond the fact that it was there and remained, sin was also acknowledged through the Law. And thus it is not understood to mean that sin existed until the Law came and then ceased to exist, but that sin received an understanding of itself which it did not possess before. And the words of the apostle clearly indicate this interpretation: "But sin was not counted where there was no law," as if to say that through the law, which it had preceded, sin was not abolished but imputed.

Yet death reigned.

It is as if he were saying that the penalty of sin, which was death, was known and recognized experientially by all men, but the cause of death, which is sin, was not recognized. Here again we ought not to understand this passage to mean that death reigned only until Moses, since Moses also died and all men do until the end of the world; and the rule of death hangs especially over those who are lost. But the expression "death reigned to Moses" means that until the time of Moses it was not understood why and whence death reigned. But Augustine understands this reign in the work cited previously, "When the guilt of sin so rules over men that it does not permit them to come to the eternal life, which is the only true life, but drags them down even to the second death (which is eternal punishment)."

In the likeness of the transgression of Adam.

Blessed Augustine, interprets this passage as applying to those who had not yet sinned in their own volition, as the other man had. Also blessed Ambrose understands the phrase "in the likeness" to refer to the preceding words "who have not sinned," for otherwise if the apostle had not defined the expression "who have not sinned" in this way, he would have contradicted his earlier statement "in which all have sinned" (v. 12). For how can it be that all have sinned and yet that some have not sinned, unless it means that all have sinned in Adam and in Adam's sin, but not all have sinned in the likeness of Adam's sin or transgression? For sin is one thing and transgression is another; for sin remains as guilt, while transgression is an act which passes on. Thus all have not sinned in action, but they are all in the same guilt; but only Adam sinned by both action and guilt insofar as he committed the first sin.

Faber Stapulensis, however, . . . understands this passage in a different way and reconciles the contradiction between the phrases "in which all have sinned" (v. 12) and "who have not sinned" (v. 14) in a different way. But I doubt, in fact, I fear, that he has not reconciled them correctly. For he refers the phrase "in the likeness" to the term "reigned," and I will accept this because of John Chrysostom, who in explaining this passage says, "How did death reign? In the likeness of Adam's transgression." And thus the phrase "even over them who have not sinned" he takes as being in a parenthetical position.

And then the expression "who have not sinned" must be understood as referring to personal sin in a stricter sense than he used above when he said "in which all have sinned." The same doctor speaks thus also of little children, "For this reason we baptize infants, even though they do not have sin," that is, actual sins of their own.

Who is a type of the One who was to come.

Chrysostom, as quoted by blessed Augustine, says concerning this passage: " 'In the likeness of the transgression of Adam, who is a type of the One who was to come,' because Adam is also a figure of Christ. And how is he a figure? they ask. The answer is that just as Adam has become a cause of death to those who are born of him, even though they have not eaten of the tree, the death brought on by the eating, so also Christ was made a provider of righteousness for those who belong to Him, even though they are entirely lacking in righteousness, and He has given it to us all through His cross."

Thus the likeness of Adam's transgression is in us, because we die, as if we had sinned in the same way he did. And the likeness of Christ's justification is in us, because we live, as if we had produced the same kind of righteousness that He did. Therefore, because of this likeness, Adam is "the type of the One who was to come," that is, Christ, who came after him. Indeed, in order that Christ might take away this likeness and give us His own, "He was born in the likeness of men" (Phil. 2:7) and sent by the Father "in the likeness of sinful flesh" (Rom. 8:3). And thus, "as in Adam all die, so also in Christ shall all be made alive" (1 Cor. 15:22). Hence I lean toward Chrysostom's view that the expression "in the likeness" ought to be connected with the word "reigned."

The free gift is not like the trespass.

Chrysostom says, "If a Jew should say to you: 'How has the world been saved by the power of the one man Christ?' you can say to him: 'How has the world been condemned by the disobedience of one man Adam?' Yet grace and sin are not equal, nor are death and life, nor God and the devil. For if sin, even the sin of one man, had such power, how can it be that the grace of God and the grace of one Man will not have greater power? For this is much more reasonable. For it certainly does not seem reasonable that one person be damned for another, but it appears much more proper and reasonable that one person be saved for another."

The grace of God and the free gift in the grace of that one Man.

The apostle joins together grace and the gift, as if they were different, but he does so in order that he may clearly demonstrate the type of the One who was to come which he has mentioned, namely, that although we are justified by God and receive His grace, yet we do not receive it by our own merit, but it is His gift, which the Father gave to Christ to give to men, according to the statement in Ephesians 4:8, "When He ascended on high, He led a host of captives, and He gave gifts to men." Therefore, these are the gifts of God's grace, which Christ received from the Father through His merit and His personal grace, in order that He might give them to us, as we read in Acts 2:33, "Having received from the Father the promise of the Holy Spirit, He has poured out this gift which you see." Thus the meaning is "the grace of God" (by which He justifies us, which actually is in Christ as in its origin, just as the sin of man is in Adam) "and the free gift," namely, that which Christ pours out from His Father upon those who believe in Him. This gift is "by the grace of that one Man," that is, by the personal merit and grace of Christ, by which He was pleasing to God, so that He might give this gift to us. This phrase "by the grace of that one Man" should be understood of the personal grace of Christ, corresponding to the personal sin of Adam which belonged to him, but the "gift" is the very righteousness which has been given to us. Thus also original sin is a gift (if I may use the term) in the sin of the one man Adam. But "the grace of God" and "the gift" are the same thing, namely, the very righteousness which is freely given to us through Christ. And He adds this grace because it is customary to give a gift to one's friends. But this gift is given even to His enemies out of His mercy, because they were not worthy of this gift unless they were made worthy and accounted as such by the mercy and grace of God.

The law came in.

He uses a very appropriate word, "came in" as if he were saying that sin entered in and the law came in on the side, that is, after sin it also entered in, and thus sin was not abolished by the law. That the Law came in on the side indicates that sin, which had come in first, still remained and was even increased. For sin entered, and the Law followed sin, arousing it by prescribing things against it and prohibiting the things which sin wished to do. Therefore, he says *that sin might abound*. This expression is not causal but consecutive, because the conjunction "that" refers to what follows and not to the final cause of the law. For the law did not come because of sin, although he also says this in Galatians 3:19, "Why then the law? It was added because of transgressions, till the seed should come to whom He made the promise." So here he uses the expression "that sin might abound," that is, for the sake of sin. Thus, the meaning is that through the transgression of the law the first sin is made known, therefore, for the sake of transgression, not in order that transgression should take place but because it necessarily followed upon the establishment of the law, so that through this transgression of the law we might learn the sinfulness of our own weakness, our blindness, and our evil desire. For it was not necessary to establish the law because of the transgression of it, inasmuch as, even if this was not the intention and if the law was not established because of transgression, yet the transgression of the law would follow, since without grace it is impossible to overcome concupiscence and to destroy the body of sin. And this affirmative statement, "the law came in, that sin might abound," is trying to show nothing else than the negative expression: the Law did not make alive, the law did not take away sin, or the law did not come in to take away sin or to make alive. Thus, this affirmative statement necessarily follows: therefore the law did come in to increase sin. And this is true, so that the meaning is [that] the law came and without any fault on the part of the law or in the intentions of the Law-giver, it happened that it came for the increasing of sin, and this happened because of the weakness of our sinful desire, which was unable to fulfill the law. Hence blessed Augustine says, "By this very word he has shown that the Jews did not understand the purpose for which the law was given. For it was not given that it might give life—for grace alone through faith gives life—but it was given to show by how many tight bonds of sin they are held who presume to fulfill the law by their own powers." This is a common method of speaking, as when a doctor comes to a sick man to console him and cannot help him because the sick man's hopes are in vain; then the sick man can say: "You have come not to comfort me but to make my despair greater." The same is the case with the law, which the human race most anxiously desires (as is evident in all the philosophers and seekers after truth), but the law is not a help and a cure; it only serves to increase the disease, as is typified by the woman in the Gospel who had the issue of blood. She had spent all her substance on doctors and yet had been made worse (Luke 8:43 ff). Hence he has used a most significant word when he says, "The law came in that sin might abound," that is, God did not establish the law for this purpose, but it became so when the law entered "that sin might abound."

During the Reformation, crucial theological debate was fiercely active. Men were put to the test as to their devotion to Christ. Luther emphasizes the need for cross-bearing, and readily acknowledges that the cross is a source of pain for those who take it up. The people of God are called upon to engage in conflict not only with flesh and blood adversaries, but also with the spiritual realm, that is, the devil. The world and the devil hate the Cross and seek to diminish its power in our lives. Luther teaches in this brief treatise the necessity of bearing with patience the cross that God bestows on an individual.

CHAPTER SEVEN

That a Christian Should Bear His Cross with Patience

The ancient and saintly fathers and theologians have contrasted the living wood with dead and have allegorized that contrast this way: From the living wood[1] came sin and death; from the dead wood,[2] righteousness and life. They conclude: do not eat from that living tree, or you will die, but eat of this dead tree; otherwise, you will remain in death.

You do indeed desire to eat and enjoy [the fruit] of some tree. I will direct you to a tree so full that you can never eat it bare. But just as it was difficult to stay away from that living tree, so it is difficult to enjoy eating from the dead tree. The first was the image of life, delight, and goodness, while the other is the image of death, suffering, and sorrow because one tree is living, the other

---

[1] I.e., the tree in the garden of Eden, Gen. 2:17.
[2] I.e., the tree of the cross on Golgotha.

dead. There is in man's heart the deeply rooted desire to seek life where there is certain death and to flee from death where one has the sure source of life.

Taking up the cross is by nature something that causes pain. It must not be self-imposed (as the Anabaptists and all the work-righteous teach); it is something that is imposed upon a person.

THE NEED FOR IT

We must be conformed to the image of the Son of God, (Rom. 8:29).

"All who desire to live a godly life in Christ Jesus will be persecuted," (2 Tim. 3:12).

"In the world you have tribulation" (John 16:33). Likewise, "You will be sorrowful; you will weep and lament, but the world will rejoice," (John 16:20).

"If we share in [Christ's] sufferings we shall also be glorified with Him," (Rom. 8:17).

"If you are left without discipline, in which all have participated, then you are illegitimate children and not sons," (Heb. 12:8). Otherwise, what is the purpose of so many comforting passages of Scripture?

THE SOURCE OF IT

The devil, a mighty, evil, deceitful spirit, hates the children of God. For them the holy cross serves for learning the faith, for [learning] the power of the Word, and for subduing whatever sin and pride remain. Indeed, a Christian can no more do without the cross than without food or drink.

THE ENTREATY

The touch of Christ sanctifies all the sufferings and sorrows of those who believe in Him. Whoever does not suffer shows that he does not believe that Christ has given him the gift of sharing in His own passion. But if anyone does not wish to bear the cross which God places upon him, he will not be compelled to do so by anyone—he is always free to deny Christ. But in so doing he must know that he cannot have fellowship with Christ or share in any of His gifts.

For example, a merchant, a hunter, a soldier risk so much pain for the sake of an uncertain gain and victory, while here, where it is certain that glory and blessedness will be the result, it is a disagreeable thing to suffer even for a bit, as Isaiah 54:7, Christ in John 16:20–22, Peter in 1 Peter 1:6, and Paul in 2 Corinthians 4:17 usually put it, "for a little while," and momentarily.

Notice how our adversaries, those torturers from the devil, are torn and divided in their teachings in so many ways that they fail to realize their hopes, since they must be concerned with so much peril and misfortune that they can never act for a moment with certainty or confidence.[3] And these penalties and punishments are only temporal! How can I comprehend their guilt, namely, that without God and through the devil's craftiness they, beset by an evil conscience, are eternally lost? Even though they are uncertain as to the outcome of their endeavor, they keep on rejoicing in a hope that is completely and absolutely lost, while we, on the other hand, have God's unfailing promises for our comfort.

In short, since God is the same and the cause is the same, in which He has upheld the faith of all the saints so that He might be vindicated, God will not now, just for our own sake, be found a liar; nor are we to make a liar of Him. God grant, whether we do or do not believe, that He

---

[3]Luther alludes here to the intrigue and cross-purposes at the Diet of Augsburg and preceding it which hindered the Roman parties from taking decisive action to root out the Lutheran heresy as they had hoped to do.

will yet defend His word and surely help [us]. This demands great effort and care so that, in the first place, we turn our eyes from the might [of this world] and second, hold fast to the Word. Eve disregarded the Word and relied on what was visible, but a Christian, in contrast, disregards what he can see and holds to the Word. The godless do not do so but rely upon the emperor to uphold them in this world, but because they neglect the Word, they will be ruined and lost to eternity.

In this devotional piece Luther examines the passion of Christ. Some think about the evil of the Jews; others feel pity for the suffering Christ. Luther felt that Christ's passion paid the penalty for sin. His suffering in our place not only delivered us from torment, but also reconciled all believers to God.

When one contemplates the work of Christ, he is made aware of his great sin. He is confronted with the guilt that has rightly been his, and with God's grace, which has paid the penalty for sin. The sins of mankind were nailed to the cross, making it possible for all men to be saved if they would only believe. The Passion represents God's great effort to reach the people who were created in His image.

✒

CHAPTER EIGHT

A Meditation on Christ's Passion

Some people meditate on Christ's passion by venting their anger on the Jews.[1] This singing and ranting about wretched Judas satisfies them, for they are in the habit of complaining about other people, of condemning and reproaching their adversaries. That might well be a meditation on the wickedness of Judas and the Jews, but not on the sufferings of Christ.

Some point to the manifold benefits and fruits that grow from contemplating Christ's passion. There is a saying ascribed to Albertus[2] about this, that it is more

---

[1]Luther's attitude toward the Jews finds frequent expression in his works. At the beginning of his career his position was one of benevolent hope of converting them to Christianity. This is reflected in this treatise, as well as in his *That Christ Was Born a Jew*, 1523. Over the years his position changed, due largely to the adamant refusal of the Jews to accept his invitation to acknowledge Christ. This is evidenced in his treatise of 1547, *On the Jews and Their Lies*.

[2]Albert Magnus (1193–1280) was a scholastic theologian, often called *"Doctor universalis,"* and a teacher of Thomas Aquinas.

beneficial to ponder Christ's passion just once than to fast a whole year or to pray a psalm daily. These people follow this saying blindly and, therefore, do not reap the fruit of Christ's passion, for in so doing they are seeking their own advantage. They carry pictures and booklets, letters and crosses on their person. Some who travel afar do this in the belief that they thus protect themselves against water and sword, fire, and all sorts of perils.[3] Christ's suffering is thus used to effect in them a lack of suffering contrary to His being and nature.

Some feel pity for Christ, lamenting and bewailing His innocence. They are like the women who followed Christ from Jerusalem and were chided and told by Christ that it would be better to weep for themselves and their children (Luke 23:27–28). They are the kind of people who go far afield in their meditation on the passion, making much of Christ's farewell from Bethany and of the Virgin Mary's anguish, but never progressing beyond that, which is why so many hours are devoted to the contemplation of Christ's passion. Only God knows whether that is invented for the purpose of sleeping or of waking.

Also to this group belong those who have learned what rich fruits the holy Mass offers. In their simplemindedness they think it enough simply to hear Mass. In support of this several teachers are cited to us who hold that the Mass is effective in itself without our merit and worthiness, and that this is all that is needed. Yet the Mass was not instituted for its own worthiness, but to make us worthy and to remind us of the passion of Christ. Where that is not done, we make of the Mass a physical and un-

---

[3]Luther here directs his criticism at those who carry holy pictures, prayer books, rosaries, etc., as amulets to ward off harm and danger, as well as those who undertake pilgrimages.

fruitful act, though even this is of some good. Of what help is it to you that God is God, if He is not God to you? Of what benefit is it to you that food and drink are good and wholesome in themselves if they are not healthful for you? And it is to be feared that many masses will not improve matters as long as we do not seek the right fruit in them.

They contemplate Christ's passion aright who view it with a terror-stricken heart and a despairing conscience. This terror must be felt as you witness the stern wrath and the unchanging earnestness with which God looks upon sin and sinners, so much so that He was unwilling to release sinners even for His only and dearest Son without His payment of the severest penalty for them. Thus He says in Isaiah 53:8, "I have chastised Him for the transgressions of My people." If the dearest child is punished thus, what will be the fate of sinners?[4] It must be an inexpressible and unbearable earnestness that forces such a great and infinite person to suffer and die to appease it. And if you seriously consider that it is God's very own Son, the eternal wisdom of the Father, who suffers, you will be terrified indeed. The more you think about it, the more intensely will you be frightened.

You must get this thought through your head and not doubt that you are the one who is torturing Christ thus, for your sins have surely wrought this. In Acts 2:36–37 Saint Peter frightened the Jews like a peal of thunder when he said to all of them, "You crucified Him." Consequently three thousand alarmed and terrified Jews asked the apostles on that one day, "O dear brethren, what shall we do now?" Therefore, when you see the

---

[4] Cf. Luke 23:31.

nails piercing Christ's hands, you can be certain that it is your work. When you behold His crown of thorns, you may rest assured that these are your evil thoughts.

For every nail that pierces Christ, more than one hundred thousand should in justice pierce you, yes, they should prick you forever and ever more painfully! When Christ is tortured by nails penetrating His hands and feet, you should eternally suffer the pain they inflict and the pain of even more cruel nails, which will in truth be the lot of those who do not avail themselves of Christ's passion. This earnest mirror,[5] Christ, will not lie or trifle, and whatever it points out will come to pass in full measure.

Saint Bernard[6] was so terrified by this that he declared, "I regarded myself secure; I was not aware of the eternal sentence that had been passed on me in heaven until I saw that God's only Son had compassion upon me and offered to bear this sentence for me. Alas, if the situation is that serious, I should not make light of it or feel secure." We read that Christ commanded the women not to weep for Him but for themselves and their children (Luke 23:28). And He adds the reason for this, saying, "For if they do this to the green wood, what will happen when it is dry?" (Luke 23:31). He says, as it were, "From My martyrdom you can learn what it is that you really deserve and what your fate should be." Here the saying applies that the small dog is whipped to frighten the big dog. Thus the prophet[7] said that all the generations on

---

[5]I.e., the one in and through whom we see our sin in its starkness.

[6]St. Bernard of Clairvaux (1090–1153), Cistercian monk, mystic, and founder of the abbey of Clairvaux, was held in high regard and frequently quoted by Luther.

[7]Cf. Jer. 4:31.

earth will bewail themselves over Him; he does not say that they will bewail Him, but that they will bewail themselves because of Him. In like manner the people of whom we heard in Acts 2:36–37 were so frightened that they said to the apostles, "O brethren, what shall we do?" This is also the song of the church: "I will ponder this diligently and, as a result, my soul will languish within me."

We must give ourselves wholly to this matter, for the main benefit of Christ's passion is that man sees into his own true self and that he be terrified and crushed by this. Unless we seek that knowledge, we do not derive much benefit from Christ's passion. The real and true work of Christ's passion is to make man conformable to Christ, so that man's conscience is tormented by his sins in like measure as Christ was pitiably tormented in body and soul by our sins. This does not call for many words but for profound reflection and a great awe of sins. Take this as an illustration: a criminal is sentenced to death for the murder of the child of a prince or a king. In the meantime you go your carefree way, singing and playing, until you are cruelly arrested and convicted of having inspired the murderer. Now the whole world closes in upon you, especially since your conscience also deserts you. You should be terrified even more by the meditation on Christ's Passion. For the evildoers, the Jews, whom God has judged and driven out, were only the servants of your sin; you are actually the one who, as we said, by his sin killed and crucified God's Son.

He who is so hardhearted and callous as not to be terrified by Christ's passion and led to a knowledge of self, has reason to fear. For it is inevitable, whether in this life or in hell, that you will have to become conformable to

Christ's image and suffering.[8] At the very least, you will sink into this terror in the hour of death and in purgatory[9] and will tremble and quake and feel all that Christ suffered on the cross. Since it is horrible to lie waiting on your deathbed, you should pray God to soften your heart and let you now ponder Christ's passion with profit to you. Unless God inspires our heart, it is impossible for us of ourselves to meditate thoroughly on Christ's passion. No meditation or any other doctrine is granted to you that you might be boldly inspired by your own will to accomplish this. You must first seek God's grace and ask that it be accomplished by His grace and not by your own power. That is why the people we referred to above fail to view Christ's passion aright. They do not seek God's help for this, but look to their own ability to devise their own means of accomplishing this. They deal with the matter in a completely human but also unfruitful way.

We say without hesitation that he who contemplates God's sufferings for a day, an hour, yes, only a quarter of an hour, does better than to fast a whole year, pray a psalm daily, yes, better than to hear a hundred masses. This meditation changes man's being and, almost like baptism, gives him a new birth. Here the passion of Christ performs its natural and noble work, strangling the old Adam and banishing all joy, delight, and confidence which man could derive from other creatures, even as Christ was forsaken by all, even by God.

Since this [strangling of the old Adam] does not rest with us, it happens that we occasionally pray for it, and

---

[8]Cf. 1 Cor. 15:49.

[9]At this point in his career Luther did not question the doctrine of purgatory.

yet do not attain it at once. Nevertheless we should neither despair nor desist. At times this happens because
we do not pray for it as God conceives of it and wishes it,
for it must be left free and unfettered. Then man becomes sad in his conscience and grumbles to himself
about the evil in his life. It may well be that he does not
know that Christ's passion, to which he gives no thought,
is effecting this in him, even as the others who do think
of Christ's passion still do not gain this knowledge of
self through it. For these the passion of Christ is hidden
and genuine, while for those it is only unreal and mis-
leading. In that way God often reverses matters, so that
those who do not meditate on Christ's passion do meditate on it, and those who do not hear Mass do hear it, and
those who hear it do not hear it.

Until now we have sojourned in Passion Week and
rightly celebrated Good Friday. Now we come to the resurrection of Christ, to the day of Easter. After man has
thus become aware of his sin and is terrified in his heart,
he must watch that sin does not remain in his conscience, for this would lead to sheer despair. Just as [our
knowledge of] sin flowed from Christ and was acknowledged by us, so we must pour this sin back on Him and
free our conscience of it. Therefore, beware, lest you do
as those perverse people who torture their hearts with
their sins and strive to do the impossible, namely, get rid
of their sins by running from one good work or penance
to another, or by working their way out of this by means
of indulgences. Unfortunately such false confidence in
penance and pilgrimages is widespread.

You cast your sins from yourself and onto Christ when
you firmly believe that His wounds and sufferings are
your sins, to be borne and paid for by Him, as we read in
Isaiah 53:6, "The Lord has laid on Him the iniquity of us

all." Saint Peter says, "In His body has He borne our sins on the wood of the cross" (1 Pet. 2:24). Saint Paul says, "God has made Him a sinner for us, so that through Him we would be made just" (2 Cor. 5:21). You must stake everything on these and similar verses. The more your conscience torments you, the more tenaciously must you cling to them. If you do not do that, but presume to still your conscience with your contrition and penance, you will never obtain peace of mind, but will have to despair in the end. If we allow sin to remain in our conscience and try to deal with it there, or if we look at sin in our heart, it will be much too strong for us and will live on forever. But if we behold it resting on Christ and [see it] overcome by His resurrection, and then boldly believe this, even it is dead and nullified. Sin cannot remain on Christ, since it is swallowed up by His resurrection. Now you see no wounds, no pain in Him, and no sign of sin. Thus Saint Paul declares that "Christ died for our sin and rose for our justification" (Rom. 4:25). That is to say, in His suffering Christ makes our sin known and thus destroys it, but through His resurrection He justifies us and delivers us from all sin, if we believe this.

If, as was said before, you cannot believe, you must entreat God for faith. This too rests entirely in the hands of God. What we said about suffering also applies here, namely, that sometimes faith is granted openly, sometimes in secret.

However, you can spur yourself on to believe. First of all, you must no longer contemplate the suffering of Christ (for this has already done its work and terrified you), but pass beyond that and see His friendly heart and how this heart beats with such love for you that it impels Him to bear with pain your conscience and your sin.

Then your heart will be filled with love for Him, and the confidence of your faith will be strengthened. Now continue and rise beyond Christ's heart to God's heart and you will see that Christ would not have shown this love for you if God in His eternal love had not wanted this, for Christ's love for you is due to His obedience to God. Thus you will find the divine and kind paternal heart, and, as Christ says, you will be drawn to the Father through Him. Then you will understand the words of Christ, "For God so loved the world that He gave His only Son" (John 3:16). We know God aright when we grasp Him not in His might or wisdom (for then He proves terrifying), but in His kindness and love. Then faith and confidence are able to exist, and then man is truly born anew in God.

After your heart has thus become firm in Christ, and love, not fear of pain, has made you a foe of sin, then Christ's passion must from that day on become a pattern for your entire life. Henceforth you will have to see His passion differently. Until now we regarded it as a sacrament which is active in us while we are passive, but now we find that we too must be active, namely, in the following. If pain or sickness afflicts you, consider how paltry this is in comparison with the thorny crown and the nails of Christ. If you are obliged to do or to refrain from doing things against your wishes, ponder how Christ was bound and captured and led hither and yon. If you are beset by pride, see how your Lord was mocked and ridiculed along with criminals. If unchastity and lust assail you, remember how ruthlessly Christ's tender flesh was scourged, pierced, and beaten. If hatred, envy, and vindictiveness beset you, recall that Christ, who indeed had more reason to avenge Himself, interceded with tears and cries for you and for all His enemies. If sadness or any adversity, physical or spiritual, distresses you, strengthen your heart and say, "Well, why should I not be willing to bear a little grief, when agonies and fears caused my Lord to sweat blood in the Garden of Gethsemane? He who lies abed while his master struggles in the throes of death is indeed a slothful and disgraceful servant."

So then, this is how we can draw strength and encouragement from Christ against every vice and feeling. That is a proper contemplation of Christ's passion, and such are its fruits. And he who exercises himself in that way does better than to listen to every story of Christ's passion or to read all the Masses. This is not to say that Masses are of no value, but they do not help us in such meditation and exercise.

Those who thus make Christ's life and name a part of their own lives are true Christians. Saint Paul says, "Those who belong to Christ have crucified their flesh with all its desires" (Gal. 5:24). Christ's passion must be met not with words or forms, but with life and truth. Thus, Saint Paul exhorts us, "Consider Him who endured such hostility from evil people against Himself, so that you may be strengthened and not be weary at heart" (Heb. 12:3). And Saint Peter, "Since therefore Christ suffered in the flesh, strengthen and arm yourselves by meditating on this" (2 Pet. 4:1). However, such meditation has become rare, although the letters of Saint Paul and Saint Peter abound with it. We have transformed the essence into semblance and painted our meditations on Christ's passion on walls and made them into letters.

Before Luther's conversion, he was a teacher and priest who was trained in theology, yet lacked a clear understanding of God's saving grace. At best he was a religious laborer whose efforts were of no redemptive value.

In this message Luther points to the flaw in thinking that the duties of religion bring salvation. He cites those who dress and act in good conscience, expecting this to lead to eternal bliss. As Luther realized for himself, it is not the outward expression of religion that makes one truly religious, nor does such conduct earn God's salvation. It is not our works that save us, but the work of Christ. He is the only means of salvation.

CHAPTER NINE

A Sermon on the Three Kinds of Good Life for the Instruction of Consciences

It should be noted first of all how God Almighty commanded through Moses in the Old Testament that a tabernacle be built and divided into three parts. The first part was the holiest part of all and was called the Holy of Holies. It was ten cubits in length, breadth, and height and cubical in shape. The next was called the Holy Place, and that was the same height and width and twenty cubits long. These two parts were joined together in one building made of wooden boards so one could go into one from the other as easily as going from one room into another. The third part was called the atrium, the courtyard, which was one hundred cubits long, fifty wide, and five high, and there was a white curtain, transparent like a net, hanging around the tabernacle. No doubt our churches have developed from this pattern. We divide them into three parts too: the churchyard, the nave, and the sanctuary. The sanctuary is the holiest, then the nave, and after that the churchyard. The same three parts are to be found in a house. First there is the yard, second the house, and third the study or bedchamber.

In this way the Holy Spirit shows that there are three kinds of preaching or teaching which make for three kinds of conscience and three kinds of sin, as well as three kinds of the good life with three kinds of good works. All these differences are helpful, and a Christian needs to know them lest he confuse one with the other and do nothing properly. He must not mistake the sanctuary for the churchyard, nor the churchyard for the nave. To understand these things better we propose to call the Holy of Holies the sanctuary, the Holy Place the nave, and the court the churchyard.

We start with the churchyard. It is preaching or teaching which is concerned only with outward works which are bound up with time and place. These matters are the ceremonies, the outward performances and techniques in matters of dress or food which cause severe damage to the conscience if a preacher does not alert his people about them. As a result of this kind of teaching, people become hardened and blind, and in this state you can tell them nothing. Let us give a few examples. Priests, monks, nuns, bishops, and all the clergy wear clothes different from the general run of people. They also do other kinds of jobs, wear sacred vestments in church, pray, sing, and so on. These are all outward works linked to dress and occasion. Now he who does these things holds that such teaching has been established by law and that they are called good works, the good life, the spiritual office. When he has done them he believes that he has most certainly earned a good conscience (for what it is worth) and that he has done the right thing. The opposite is true too—if he overlooks one of them or neglects to do it, for example, if he does not wear his garb properly or does not observe the [canonical] hours, he gets a bad conscience like a man who has not kept the commandments.

We act the same way when we observe or break the prescribed commandments, fasts, and feasts, until, through the neglect of the clergy, who are asleep on the job, we reach the point where we make it a more serious matter of conscience for someone to eat a morsel of bread on the eve of a fast than to soak himself in drink, or curse and swear, lie, deceive, or commit adultery or some other serious sin, so inseparably does this kind of teaching bind life and conscience to food and external things. In fact today there are many clergy who would have pangs of conscience ten times worse if they were to celebrate the Mass without a maniple or a chasuble or an altar stone[1] or a silver chalice and things like that, than if they had spoken five times in a scurrilous and scandalous fashion or told lies or spoken behind somebody's back, or otherwise injured their neighbor, so inseparably bound up with these external things is their conscience and so far removed from the things that matter. And what layman or man in the street does not endure worse pangs of conscience if he eats eggs or butter or meat on the eve of a saint's day or other fast day than if he had killed or been unchaste by word or deed? Yes, things are in such a state, owing to certain blind teachers, that no layman dare touch the chalice or corporal. A great fuss and matter of conscience is made of it if anybody unwittingly does touch it. It is worse than that! If an ordinary man were incautiously to touch the holy sac-

---

[1]Luther is referring to the marble tablets carried about by clergy, on which mass was celebrated when no episcopally consecrated altar was available, e.g., on military expeditions.

rament with his finger, they skin that finger for him. They make such a matter of conscience out of this affair that there is not a command or prohibition that I regard, they have become so ridiculous.

Just think it over. Such a view of conscience and such error arise from the fact that people have got everything confused and do not differentiate one thing from another in the right way. Then sound instruction and the capacity to differentiate are gone, and before we know where we are, we have reached the stage where the worst is upheld as the best, and the best as the worst. Then the fear of God goes out, human presumption takes over, and the hardening and blinding of men to their sins goes on apace. This is easy to see everywhere in the world. Is it not true that everybody, spiritual and secular estate alike, is unfaithful, prideful, avaricious, hateful, unchaste, and commits all the sins there are, and that nobody takes the slightest notice of them? They have the audacity to think that they live in the fear of the Lord and do His works, although they do not seek to improve themselves in these particular items. They think that they are in a right relationship with God, and that they are doing quite well so long as they exercise their office, pray the canonical hours, wear their clerical garb, and do the right thing in church.

The laity think the same, that all they have to do is to keep their fasts and feasts. As if our God were bothered in the slightest whether you drink beer or water, whether you eat fish or meat, whether you keep the feasts or fasts! It was of people like this that Christ spoke in Matthew 23:23–24, "Woe to you, scribes and Pharisees, hypocrites! for you tithe mint and dill and cummin, and have neglected the weightier matters of the law, justice and mercy and faith; these you ought to have done, without neglecting the others. You blind guides, straining out a gnat and swallowing a camel!"

Has our Lord Himself not depicted here the foolish, perverted conscience which offends God by making important matters trifles and trifles important? How is it that a man can take such a careful sip of outward works that he even strains out a gnat, and can take such a gulp of the right works that he even swallows a camel? It is because he makes things which matter little if at all into strict matters of conscience, but has a very free and easy conscience in things of great importance on which everything depends. People who do this are all churchyard saints. They are only five cubits high. This means that their holiness is circumscribed by their five senses and their bodily existence. And yet, this very holiness shines brighter in the eyes of the world than does real holiness. That is why many stand in this court, for the churchyard is more than three times the length of the nave and ten times as long as the sanctuary. Further, the fact that there are such vast numbers in the courtyard constitutes a great inducement to follow such erroneous, perverted ideas of conscience, works, and life. Indeed, the office of the preacher and pastor is a very serious matter, for the clergy will have to render a solemn account of their failure here if they are not vigilant and active now, and are not striving against such a state of affairs and giving their people true instruction in these matters. But there is another side to it. If they resolve to do this, they will have to suffer persecution from the pope, the bishops, and the prelates. For that gang is itself in such a "churchyardish" state of spiritual life, utterly drowned in grave sin, that they will not let anyone teach anything different. They want to strain gnats and swallow camels.

Anybody can see for himself that such a "churchyardish" external system betters nobody, and that all the performances bound up with food and clothes, occasion and place, make nobody righteous. For everybody can see that such people continue to be unfaithful, avaricious, impatient, proud, unchaste, angry, and envious. In fact, nobody is more deeply involved in those sins than these very people who have equated righteousness with matters of food, clothing, and observances of time and place. We can see this all around us. Is it not time we called a halt and thought things over? This cannot be the right road to become righteous. There must be another way somewhere. And because these people take such a light view of transgressing in very serious matters, we ought to be wise enough to despise the transgressions of their external pomposities in which we see so much that is corrupt. We must get into the habit of looking in the right direction.

Imagine you were to meet a slanderer or a vulgar gossip, and then you were to meet another man who happened not to have kept the fast or feast or who had eaten nonprescribed food. Would you not be ten times more shocked by the first man than by the second? Would you not regard the second man as one who had swallowed a gnat, and the first a camel? It is grievous and aggravating that the pope is so concerned about eating butter and eggs that people have to buy letters from him, and yet at the same time he is not bothered about whether a man sins against God. The bishops and the prelates follow suit in this, and aid and abet him. If they themselves confuse these matters and get them upside-down, strain gnats and swallow camels, how shall the poor people extricate themselves? How indeed, when their rulers and teachers fight against them in this by their doctrine, example, and authority?

Let us now leave the atrium or churchyard and proceed into the Holy Place, the nave. This means teaching, works, and concepts of conscience which are really good. These are humility, meekness, gentleness, peace, fidelity, love, propriety, purity, and the like. These are not bound up with food and clothing, or with place, time, or person. For in these matters a layman may do more of value than a priest, a priest more than a pope, a woman more than a man, a boy more than an adult, a poor man more than a rich man, a naked man more than a man richly clad; more of value may be done in the field than in the home, more in the secret chamber than in the church. This is what God looks for. He who takes this course is traveling on the right road to heaven, apart from what he does or leaves undone in the atrium, for God does not ask him about what happened there, so long as he journeys rightly in this holy place. On the other hand, it is in the nave that we ought to make it a matter of conscience if anybody blasphemes, swears, or speaks uncleanly, or if anybody hears, sees, does, or thinks anything improper. That constitutes the true conscience. It is here that a man strains camels and swallows gnats. It is here that a man gathers up the corn and casts away the chaff. It is here that Abel sacrifices a lamb and lets Cain sacrifice his straw. It is here that a man must fight against pride, avarice, immodesty, anger, hatred, and the like. Here must we keep ourselves fully occupied as long as we live, so as to forget the churchyard altogether and not want it. Here we see what is the proper road to piety and holiness, for we see for ourselves that those who practice this become truly righteous, but those who practice "churchyard" piety do not. That proves that this way and not the other must be the right way.

Some do these works in a living and selfless way. Others, however, set about them in the wrong way. They drag their dead works in with them on their backs and bury them. These are the ones who maintain a pious posture not of their own desire, but because they fear disgrace, punishment, or hell. For many a man is chaste. But if there were no shame or punishment attached to unchastity, then they would go in for it just like those who pay no regard to shame or punishment. In a similar way, many a man controls his anger or temper not gladly or because he loves gentleness, but because he could not very well vent his anger and does not like to confess it. Many a man even gives to the church and endows services, not from generosity but for the sake of glory or to satisfy his vanity. And this false ground is so deep that no saint has ever fathomed its bottom, but shows uncertainty about it and says, "Lord God, create in me a clean heart, and renew a right spirit or will in my inmost being" (Ps. 51:10). Or again in Psalm 19:12, "Lord, who can know all his faults? Cleanse me from secret sins." God does not just want such works by themselves. He wants them to be performed gladly and willingly. And when there is no joy in doing them, and the right will and motive are absent, then they are dead in God's eyes. Such work is riddled with errors; it is service under compulsion, necessity, and duress and is not pleasing to God. As Saint Paul says, "God loves a cheerful giver" (2 Cor. 9:7).

Such gladness, love, joy, and willingness are not found in the heart of any man on earth. As far as our nature goes, we are all sinners. We do not really want to be righteous; we only pretend because we are afraid of being punished or disgraced, or because we seek our own ends and pleasure in these works. And no one is righteous solely and alone for God's sake, the way it ought to be.

The natural man wants to and has to seek something whereby he may be righteous; he is not able and has no desire to be righteous for righteousness' sake. He does not allow himself to be content with righteousness, as he ought to do, but is determined by means of it either to earn something or escape something. But that is wrong in God's sight. As Saint Paul concludes in Romans 3:10, quoting Psalm 14:1, "Therefore no man is righteous in God's sight." We ought not be good to earn something or avoid something, for that is to behave no better than a hireling, a bondsman, a journeyman, and not as willing children and heirs who are righteous for the sake of righteousness itself. Children and heirs are righteous only for righteousness' sake, that is, for God's own sake alone, for God Himself is righteousness, truth, goodness, wisdom, holiness. He who seeks nothing other than holiness is the one who seeks God Himself, and he will find Him. He who seeks reward, however, and avoids pain, never finds Him at all and makes reward his god. Whatever it is that makes a man do something, that motive is his god.

For these reasons man has to go down on his knees for grace and deny himself. To this end, then, God has built the sanctuary and *Sanctum sanctorum*[2] for us. Here He has set Christ before us and promised that he who believes in Him and calls on His name shall at once receive the Holy Spirit. As He says in John 16, "The Father will send the Holy Spirit in My name."[3] A man who denies himself and calls upon Christ in genuine trust is certain to receive the Holy Spirit. Where Christ's name is, there the Holy Spirit follows. He who calls on Christ in faith,

---

[2]Holy of Holies.
[3]A conflation of John 16:7 and 26.

however, possesses His name, and the Holy Spirit most certainly comes to Him. When the Spirit comes, however, He makes a pure, free, cheerful, glad, and loving heart, a heart which is simply gratuitously, righteous, seeking no reward, fearing no punishment. Such a heart is holy for the sake of holiness and righteousness alone and does everything with joy. Look! Here is really sound doctrine! This shows what a conscience is and what good works are! It is to go into the *Sanctum sanctorum*,[4] to pass into the sanctuary. That is the last thing on earth that any man can do. This is the road to heaven. No man remains wicked; on the contrary, all become righteous. This road is quite the opposite of the atrium, for it has no regard for the external things of the churchyard. Indeed, one sees only what enemies of this road they are and how dangerous they are.

Christ referred to this when he said in Mark 16:16, "He that believes shall be saved." Faith alone saves. Why? Faith brings with it the Spirit, and He performs every good work with joy and love. In this way the Spirit fulfills God's commandments, and brings a man his salvation, all of which is signified by the sanctuary and the nave (the *Sanctum* and the *Sanctum sanctorum*)[5] being built in one and the same structure. But the atrium, the churchyard that lies apart, is to show that good works without faith cannot happen, and that faith without works cannot endure. A preacher should not try to separate the two, although he should push faith to the fore. Further, faith and good works may well exist without the continuance of those external things, such as sacred foods, sacred garments, sacred times, sacred places. It is

---

[4] Holy of Holies.
[5] "Holy" and "Holy of Holies."

for this reason that it is written in the Apocalypse that in the new dispensation the court would be handed over to the heathen (Rev. 11:2), because in the new covenant external matters of this kind should rest with the free and unfettered choice of each individual. Consequently, only the nave and the sanctuary would really be used.

Tragically has it come to pass that there has never been a people on the face of the earth that has had a bitter atrium, more holy foods, more holy garments, more holy days, more holy places, than Christians now have! It is the fault of the pope and of his canon law, in which so many worthless, dangerous, and aggravating regulations are laid down to the unspeakable detriment and obscuring of faith and good works. May God redeem us from them and protect us with His grace. Amen.

The letters of Martin Luther serve as windows to the heart of a man who on the outside seemed hard but who, inwardly, had a deep sense of tenderness toward his loved ones. His letters reveal a side of Luther many have never seen. These letters show us Martin Luther as husband, father, and child.

Luther the husband is shown to be loving and deeply appreciative of his wife. It is clear that she played an important role in his life as counselor, sounding board, and comforter. Such letters are good examples of how a minister should involve his wife in his life and ministry.

Luther the father is deeply concerned about the welfare of his children. He is constantly encouraging them to love God and never lose sight of His importance. We also find him involved in their education. He praises them for good study habits and conduct. This age is unaccustomed to seeing Christian men so involved with their children.

Finally, Luther the son never lost his love for his parents and always sought to keep them informed of his activities. He honored his parents and saw to it that they knew how important they were to him.

Luther's letters illustrate how Christians should regulate their domestic lives. In doing so they develop a heritage that will either be a curse or blessing.

CHAPTER TEN

Letters

TO HANS LUTHER

This book[1] I have decided to dedicate to you, dearest father. [I do not intend to make] your name famous in the world and to glory in the flesh, which would be contrary to the teaching of Saint Paul.[2] Rather my purpose is to recall, in a short preface, what took place between you and me in order to indicate to the pious reader the argument and the content of this book, together with an example.

To begin with, I wish you to know that your son has reached the point where he is altogether persuaded that there is nothing holier, nothing more important, nothing

---

[1] *Martin Luther's Opinion on Monastic Vows* (Wittenberg: M. Lotther, February, 1522).
[2] Gal. 6:13.

more scrupulously to be observed than God's commandment.[3] But here you will say, "Have you been so so unfortunate as ever to doubt this, and have you only now learned that this is so?" Most unfortunately indeed, I not only doubted it, but I did not at all know that it is so; and if you will permit me, I am ready to show you that this ignorance was common to both of us.

It is now almost sixteen years since I became a monk,[4] taking the vow without your knowledge and against your will. In your paternal love you were fearful about my weakness because I was then a youth, just entering my twenty-second year (that is, to use Saint Augustine's words, I was still "clothed in hot youth"),[5] and you had learned from numerous examples that this way of life turned out sadly for many. You were determined, therefore, to tie me down with an honorable and wealthy marriage.[6] This fear of yours, this care, this indignation against me was for a time implacable. [Your] friends tried in vain to persuade you that if you wished to offer something to God, you ought to give your dearest and your best. The Lord, meanwhile, was dinning in your ears that Psalm verse: "God knows the thoughts of men, that they are vain";[7] but you were deaf. At least you desisted and bowed to the will of God, but your fears for

---

[3]In this case the Fourth Commandment.

[4]Luther entered the monastery in July of 1505.

[5]St. Augustine's *Confessions* (see *Patrology*, pp. 499 f.), II, 3.

[6]As far as this editor can see, this seems to be the only reference from which the marriage plans his father had for Luther can be deduced. These plans seem to be quite in agreement with the father's ambition to see young Martin in the important and influential position of a legally-trained administrator.

[7]Ps. 94:11 (Vulgate).

me were never laid aside. For I remember very well[8] that after we were reconciled and you were [again] talking with me, I told you that I had been called by terrors from heaven and that I did not become a monk of my own free will and desire, still less to gain any gratification of the flesh, but that I was walled in by the terror and the agony of sudden death and forced by necessity to take the vow. Then you said, "Let us hope that it was not an illusion and a deception." That word penetrated to the depths of my soul and stayed there, as if God had spoken by your lips, though I hardened my heart against you and your word as much as I could. You said something else too. When in filial confidence I upbraided you for your wrath, you suddenly retorted with a reply so fitting and so much to the point that I have hardly ever in all my life heard any man say anything which struck me so forcibly and stayed with me so long. "Have you not also heard," you said, "that parents are to be obeyed?" But I was so sure of my own righteousness that in you I heard only a man and boldly ignored you; though in my heart I could not ignore your word.

See now, whether you too were not unaware that the commandments of God are to be put before all things. If you had known that I was then in your power, would you not have used your paternal authority to pull me out of the cowl? On the other hand, had I known it, I would never have attempted to become a monk without your knowledge and consent, even though I had to die many deaths. For my vow was not worth a fig, since by taking it I withdrew myself from the authority and guidance of

---

[8]The following is a recollection of what took place between father and son at the celebration of Luther's first mass.

the parent [to whom I was subject] by God's commandment; indeed, it was a wicked vow and proved that it was
not of God not only because it was a sin against your
authority, but because it was not absolutely free and vol-
untary.[9] In short it was taken in accordance with the doctrines of men and the superstition of hypocrites, none of
which God has commanded. But behold how much good
God (whose mercies are without number and whose wisdom is without end)[10] has made to come out of all these
errors and sins! Would you now not rather have lost a
hundred sons than not have seen this good?

I think that from [the days of] my childhood Satan
must have foreseen something in me [which is the cause]
of his present suffering. He has therefore raged against
me with incredible contrivings to destroy or hinder me,
so that I have often wondered whether I was the only
man in the whole world whom he was seeking. But it was
the Lord's will, as I now see, that the wisdom of the
schools and the sanctity of the monasteries should become known to me by my own actual experience, that is,
through many sins and impieties, so that wicked men
might not have a chance, when I became their adversary,
to boast that I condemned something about which I
knew nothing. Therefore, I lived as a monk, indeed not
without sin but without reproach. For in the kingdom
of the pope, impiety and sacrilege pass for supreme
piety; still less are they considered matters for
reproach.

What do you think now? Will you still take me out of
the monastery? You are still my father, and I am still

---

[9]I.e., the vow was said under the pressure of external circumstances (the
lightning near Stotternheim) and thus with the wrong motivation.
[10]Ps. 147:5.

your son, and all the vows are worthless. On your side is the authority of God; on my side there is nothing but human presumption. For that continence of which they boast with puffed-up cheeks is valueless without obedience to God's commandments. Continence is not commanded but obedience is, yet the mad and silly papists will not allow any virtue to be equal to continence and virginity. They extol both these virtues with such prodigious lies that their very craze for lying and the greatness of their ignorance, singly or together, ought to cast suspicion on all they do or think.

What kind of intelligence do they show when they distort the word of the sage, "No balance can weigh the value of a continent mind," to mean that virginity and continence are to be preferred to everything else and that vows of virginity cannot be commuted or dispensed with? It was a Jew who wrote these words to Jews about a chaste wife; among the Jews virginity and continence were condemned. Thus, too, they apply to virgins that eulogy of a modest wife: "This is she who has not known a sinful bed."[11] In a word, although the Scriptures do not laud virginity but only approve it, these men,[12] who are so ready to inflame men's souls to lives that endanger their salvation, dress it up in borrowed plumes, so to speak, by applying to it the praises the Scriptures bestow on a chaste marriage.

But isn't [the value] of an obedient soul also beyond all measure? For that reason indeed a continent soul (that is, a chaste wife) defies every measure, not only because [such a soul] is commanded by God but also because, as the well-known proverb says, there is nothing in the

---

[11] Wisdom of Solomon 3:13.
[12] I.e., the papists.

world more desirable than a chaste wife.[13] But these "faithful" interpreters of Scripture [take] everything that is said about the continence which is commanded [and] apply it to that type of continence which is not commanded and make a human evaluation the measure of God's judgment. Thus, they grant dispensations from everything, even from obedience to God, [but they grant no dispensation from continence],[14] even from that forbidden continence which is entered upon against the authority of one's parents. O worthy and truly picayunish papistic doctors and teachers! Virginity and chastity are to be praised, but in such a way that by their very greatness men are frightened off from them rather than led to them. This was Christ's way. When the disciples praised continence and said, "If such is the case of a man with his wife, it is expedient not to marry," He at once set their minds straight on the matter and said, "Not all men can receive this precept."[15] The precept must be accepted, but it was Christ's will that only a few should understand it.

But to come back to you, my father; would you still take me out of the monastery? But that you would not boast of it, the Lord has anticipated you and taken me out Himself. What difference does it make whether I retain or lay aside the cowl and tonsure? Do [they] make the monk? "All things are yours, and you are Christ's," says Paul.[16] Shall I belong to the cowl, or shall not the cowl rather belong to me? My conscience has been freed,

---

[13]This is either a popular saying (which could not be traced) or an allusion to Prov. 12:4; 31:10, 30.

[14]I.e., the monastic and clerical vow of celibacy.

[15]Matt. 19:10–11.

[16]1 Cor. 3:22–23.

and that is the most complete liberation. Therefore, I am still a monk and yet not a monk. I am a new creature, not of the pope but of Christ. The pope also has his creatures, but he creates puppets and straw-men, that is, masks and idols of himself. I myself was formerly one of them, led astray by the various usages of words, by which even the sage confesses that he was brought into the danger of death but by God's grace was delivered.[17]

But am I not robbing you again of your right and authority? No, for your authority over me still remains, so far as the monastic life is concerned; but this is nothing to me anymore, as I have said. Nevertheless, [God], who has taken me out of the monastery, has an authority over me that is greater than yours; you see that He has placed me now not in a pretended monastic service but in the true service of God. Who can doubt that I am in the ministry of the Word? And it is plain that the authority of parents must yield to this service, for Christ says, "He who loves father or mother more than Me is not worthy of Me."[18] Not that this word destroys the authority of parents, for the Apostle [Paul] often insists that children should obey their parents;[19] but if the authority of parents conflicts with the authority or calling of Christ, then Christ's authority must reign alone.

Therefore—so I am now absolutely persuaded—I could not have refused to obey you without endangering my conscience unless [Christ] had added the ministry of the Word to my monastic profession. This is what I meant when I said that neither you nor I realized that

---

[17]Ecclesiasticus 34:12–13.
[18]Matt. 10:37.
[19]Eph. 6:1; Col. 3:20.

God's commandments must be put before everything else. But almost the whole world is now laboring under this same ignorance, for under the papal abomination error rules. So Paul also predicted when he said that men would become disobedient to parents. This fits the monks and priests exactly, especially those who under the pretense of piety and the guise of serving God withdraw themselves from the authority of their parents, as though there were any other service of God except the keeping of His commandments, which includes obedience to parents.

I am sending [you] this book, then, in which you may see by what signs and wonders Christ has absolved me from the monastic vow and granted me such great liberty. Although He has made me the servant of all men, I am, nevertheless, subject to no one except to Him alone. He is Himself (as they say) my immediate bishop,[20] abbot, prior, lord, father, and teacher; I know no other. Thus, I hope that He has taken from you one son in order that He may begin to help the sons of many others through me. You ought not only to endure this willingly, but you ought to rejoice with exceeding joy—and this I am sure is what you will do. What if the pope should slay me or condemn me to the depths of hell! Having once slain me, he will not raise me up again to slay me a second and third time, and now that I have been condemned I have no desire ever to be absolved. I trust that the day is at hand when that kingdom of abomination and perdition will be destroyed. Would that we were worthy to be burned or slain by him[21] before that time, so that our

---

[20]I.e., the diocesan bishop to whom the individual church member was subordinate.

[21]I.e., the pope, or Satan.

blood might cry out against him all the more and hasten the day of his judgment! But if we are not worthy to bear testimony with our blood, then let us at least pray and implore mercy that we may testify with deed and word that Jesus Christ alone is the Lord our God, who is praised forever. Amen.

Farewell, [in the Lord], my dearest father, and greet in Christ my mother, your Margaret, and our whole family.

From the wilderness, Wartburg, November 21, 1521
Dedication of On Monastic Vows

TO JOHN LUTHER

Grace and peace in Christ! My beloved son, I am pleased to learn that you are doing well in your studies, and that you are praying diligently. Continue to do so, my son, [and] when I return home I shall bring you a nice present from the fair.

I know of a pretty, beautiful, [and] cheerful garden where there are many children wearing little golden coats. [They] pick up fine apples, pears, cherries, [and] yellow and blue plums under the trees; they sing, jump, and are merry. They also have nice ponies with golden reins and silver saddles. I asked the owner of the garden whose children they were. He replied, "These are the children who like to pray, study, and be good." Then I said, "Dear sir, I also have a son, whose name is Hänschen Luther. Might he not also [be permitted] to enter the garden, so that he too could eat such fine apples and pears, and ride on these pretty ponies, and play with these children?" Then the man answered, "If he too likes to pray, study, and be good, he too may enter the garden, and also Lippus and Jost. And when they are all together [there], they will also get whistles, drums, lutes, and all kinds of other stringed instruments; and they will also dance and shoot with little crossbows." And he showed me there a lovely lawn in the garden, all prepared for dancing, where many gold whistles and drums and fine silver crossbows were hanging. But it was still so early [in the morning] that the children had not yet eaten; therefore, I couldn't wait for the dancing. So I said to the man, "Dear sir, I shall hurry away and write about all this to my dear son Hänschen so that he will certainly study hard, pray diligently, and be good in order that he too may get into this garden. But he has an Aunt Lena, whom he must bring along." "By all means," said the man, "go and write him accordingly."

Therefore, dear son Hänschen, do study and pray diligently, and tell Lippus and Jost to study and pray too; then you [boys] will get into the garden together. Herewith, I commend you to the dear Lord ['s keeping]. Greet Aunt Lena, and give her a kiss for me.

June 19, 1530   Your loving father,
Coburg   MARTIN LUTHER

TO MRS. MARGARET LUTHER

My dearly beloved[22] mother! I have received my brother James's[23] letter concerning your illness. Of course this grieves me deeply, especially because I cannot be with you in person, as I certainly would like to be. Yet I am coming to you personally through this letter, and I, together with all the members of my family, shall certainly not be absent from you in spirit.

---

[22]Literally: "Beloved from the heart [or: heartily beloved]."
[23]James Luther.

260

I trust that you have long since been abundantly instructed, without any help from me, that (God be praised) you have taken [God's] comforting Word into [your heart], and that you are adequately provided with preachers and comforters. Nevertheless, I shall do my part too and, according to my duty, acknowledge myself to be your child, and you to be my mother, as our common God and Creator has made us and bound us to each other with mutual ties, so that I shall in this way increase the number of your comforters.

First, dear mother, by God's grace you well know by now that this sickness of yours is [God's] fatherly, gracious chastisement.[24] It is a quite small chastisement in comparison with that which He inflicts upon the godless and, sometimes, even His own dear children, when one person is beheaded, another burned, a third drowned, and so on.[25] And so all of us must sing, "For Thy sake we are being daily killed and regarded as sheep to be slaughtered."[26] This sickness, therefore, should not distress or depress you. On the contrary, you should accept it with thankfulness as being sent by God's grace; [you should] recognize how slight a suffering it is—even if it be a sickness unto death—compared with the sufferings of His own dear Son, our Lord Jesus Christ, who did not have to suffer on behalf of Himself, as we have to do, but who suffered for us and for our sins.

Second, dear mother, you also know the true center and foundation of your salvation from whom you are to seek comfort in this and all troubles, namely, Jesus

---

[24]See Heb. 12:6, 11; Rev. 3:19.
[25]This is perhaps a reference to the persecutions suffered by some of the evangelicals.
[26]Ps. 44:22; Rom. 8:36.

Christ, the cornerstone.[27] He will not waver or fail us, nor allow us to sink or perish, for He is the Savior and is called the Savior of all poor sinners, and of all who are caught in tribulation and death, and rely on Him, and call on His name.

[Christ] says, "Be of good cheer; I have overcome the world."[28] If He has overcome the world, surely He has also overcome the sovereign of this world[29] with all his power. But what else is [the devil's] power but death, by which he has made us subject to himself, [and] held us captives on account of our sin? But now that death and sin are overcome, we may joyfully and cheerfully listen to the sweet words: "Be of good cheer; I have overcome the world." We certainly are not to doubt that these words are indeed true. More than that, we are commanded to accept this comfort with joy and thanksgiving. Whoever would be unwilling to be comforted by these words would do the greatest injustice and dishonor to the dear Comforter, as if it were not true that He bids us to be of good cheer, or as if it were not true that He has overcome the world. [If we acted thus,] we would only restore within ourselves the tyranny of the vanquished devil, sin and death, and oppose the dear Savior. From this may God preserve us.

Let us, therefore, now rejoice with all assurance and gladness, and should any thought of sin or death frighten us, let us in opposition to this lift up our hearts and say, "Behold, dear soul, what are you doing? Dear death, dear sin, how is it that you are alive and terrify me? Do you not know that you have been overcome? Do

[27]See 1 Pet. 2:6; Isa. 28:16.
[28]John 16:33.
[29]See John 12:31.

you, death, not know that you are quite dead? Do you not know the One who says of you, 'I have overcome the world'? It does not behoove me either to listen to your terrifying suggestions, or heed them. Rather [I should listen] to the comforting words of my Savior: 'Be of good cheer, be of good cheer; I have overcome the world.' He is the victor, the true hero, who gives and appropriates to me His victory with this word: 'Be of good cheer!' I shall cling to Him, and to His words and comfort I shall hold fast; regardless whether I remain here or go yonder, I shall live by [this word, for] He does not lie to me. You would like to deceive me with your terrors, and with your lying thoughts you would like to tear me away from such a victor and Savior. But they are lies, as surely as it is true that He has overcome you and commanded us to be comforted.

"Saint Paul also boasts likewise and defies the terrors of death: 'Death is swallowed up in victory. O death, where is thy victory? O hell, where is thy sting?'[30] Like a wooden image of death, you can terrify and challenge, but you have no power to strangle. For your victory, sting, and power have been swallowed up in Christ's victory. You can show your teeth, but you cannot devour, for God has given us the victory over you through Christ Jesus our Lord, to whom be praise and thanks. Amen."

By such words and thoughts, and by none other, let your heart be moved, dear mother. Above all be thankful that God has brought you to such knowledge and not allowed you to remain caught in papistic error, by which we were taught to rely on our own works and the holi-

---

[30]See 1 Cor. 15:54 f.

ness of the monks, and to consider this only comfort of ours, our Savior, not as a comforter but as a severe judge and tyrant, so that we had to flee from Him to Mary and the saints, and not expect of Him any grace or comfort. But now we know it differently; [we know] about the unfathomable goodness and mercy of our heavenly Father: that Jesus Christ is our mediator,[31] our throne of grace,[32] and our bishop[33] before God in heaven, who daily intercedes for us and reconciles all who believe in Him alone, and who call upon Him;[34] that He is not a judge, nor cruel, except for those who do not believe in Him, or who reject His comfort and grace; [and] that He is not the man who accuses and threatens us, but rather the man who reconciles us [with God], and intercedes for us with His own death and blood shed for us so that we should not fear Him, but approach Him with all assurance and call Him dear Savior, sweet Comforter, faithful bishop of our souls.

To such knowledge (I say) God has graciously called you. You possess God's seal and letter of this [calling], namely, the gospel you hear preached, baptism, and the sacrament of the altar,[35] so that you should have no trouble or danger. Only be of good cheer and thank [God] joyfully for such great grace! For He who has begun [His work] in you will also graciously complete it,[36] since we are unable to help ourselves in such matters. We are un-

---

[31]1 Tim. 2:5.

[32]Rom. 3:25 (Luther Bible); Heb. 4:16.

[33]1 Pet. 2:25 (Luther Bible).

[34]Rom. 8:34; 1 Tim. 4:10; Heb. 7:25.

[35]Literally: "the gospel, baptism, and sacrament, which you hear being preached."

[36]Phil. 1:6.

able to accomplish anything against sin, death, and the devil by our own works. Therefore, another appears for us and in our stead who definitely can do better; He gives us His victory, and commands us to accept it and not to doubt it. He says, "Be of good cheer; I have overcome the world"; and again: "I live, and you will live also, and no one will take your joy from you."[37]

The Father and God of all consolation[38] grant you, through His holy Word and Spirit, a steadfast, joyful, and grateful faith blessedly to overcome this and all other trouble, and finally to taste and experience that what He Himself says is true: "Be of good cheer; I have overcome the world." And with this I commend your body and soul to His mercy. Amen.

All your children and my Katie pray for you; some weep, others say at dinner, "Grandmother is very sick." God's grace be with us all. Amen.

May 20, 1531   Your loving son,
Wittenberg   MARTIN LUTHER

TO MRS. KATHARINE LUTHER

God in Christ be with you! My dearly beloved Katie! As soon as Doctor Brück is granted permission to leave the court—he puts me off with this prospect—I hope to come along with him tomorrow or the next day. Pray God to bring us home chipper and healthy! I am sleeping very well, about six or seven hours without interruption, and then thereafter again for two or three hours. It's the

---

[37] John 14:19; 16:22.
[38] Rom. 15:5 (Luther Bible).

beer's fault, I think. But, just as in Wittenberg, I am sober.

Doctor Caspar[39] says that the gangrene in our Gracious Lord's[40] foot will spread no further.[41] But neither Dobitzsch[42] nor any prisoner on the stretching rack in jail suffers such agony from John the jailer as His Electoral Grace suffers from the surgeons. His Sovereign Grace is, in his whole body, as healthy as a little fish, but the devil has bitten and pierced His Grace's foot. Pray, and continue to pray! I trust God will listen to us, as He has begun. For Doctor Caspar too thinks that in this case God has to help.

Since John[43] is moving away, it is both necessary and honorable that I let him go honorably from me. For you know that he has served me faithfully and diligently and conducted himself with humility, and [he has] done and endured all [he was required to do], according to the gospel. Remember how often we have given something to bad boys and ungrateful students, in which cases all that we did was lost. Now, therefore, reach into your wallet[44] and let nothing be lacking for this fine fellow, since you know that it is well used and God-pleasing. I certainly

---

[39]I.e., Dr. Caspar Lindemann, the Elector's personal physician.

[40]I.e., Elector John.

[41]Literally: "that our Gracious Lord's foot will not eat further."

[42]This is a reference to an infamous outlaw knight who had been executed on November 30, 1531.

[43]I.e., John Rischmann of Brunswick. He had studied in Wittenberg since 1527, had been Luther's *famulus,* and had lived with the Luther family. With Luther's fine letter of recommendation, dated February 27, 1532, Rischmann became assistant principal of a school in Husum (Schleswig-Holstein) in 1533; soon thereafter he was appointed deacon and archdeacon there. In 1544 he visited Luther again in order to get advice on a marital problem of one of his parishioners.

[44]Literally: "So, now touch yourself here [i.e., in this case]."

know that little is available; yet if I had them I wouldn't mind giving him ten gulden. But you shouldn't give him less than five gulden, since we didn't give him a new suit of clothes [upon his departure]. Whatever you might be able to do beyond this, do it, I beg you for it. The Common Chest might, of course, make a present to my servant in my honor, in view of the fact that I am forced to maintain my servants at my expense for the service and benefit of the local congregation.[45] But they may do as they please. Yet under no circumstances should you let anything be lacking as long as there is still a fine goblet [in the house]. Figure out from where you will take the money. God certainly will provide more; this I know. With this I commend you to God. Amen.

Tell the pastor of Zwickau he really ought to be pleased and content with the quarters. Upon my return I shall tell you how Mühlpfort and I have been guests of Rietesel, and how Mühlpfort has demonstrated much wisdom to me. But I wasn't eager for his wisdom.

Kiss young Hans for me,[46] keep after Hänschen, Lenchen,[47] and Aunt Lena to pray for the dear Sovereign and for me. I am unable to find anything to buy for the children in this town even though there is now a fair here. If I am unable to bring anything special along, please have something ready for me!

February 27, 1532   DOCTOR MARTIN LUTHER
Torgau

---

[45]Literally: "benefit of their [i.e., the citizens of Wittenberg] church."
[46]John Luther
[47]Magdalen Luther

TO JOHN LUTHER

Thus far, my dearest son, your studies and the letters you have written to me have been a pleasure for me. If you continue this way then not only will you please me, your father who loves you, but you also will very much benefit yourself, so that you will not seem to have stained yourself with dishonor. Therefore, take care to pursue diligently what you started. For God, who has commanded children to be obedient to their parents, has also promised His blessing to obedient children. See to it that you have only this blessing before your eyes and that you do not let yourself be diverted from it by any evil example. For that same God has also threatened disobedient children with a curse. Therefore, fear God who blesses and curses, who even though He delays with His promises and threats, a fact which leads to the ruin of the evil, nevertheless, quite quickly implements them for the well-being of the good. Fear God, therefore, and listen to your parents—who certainly want nothing but the best for you—and run from disgraceful and disreputable conversations.

Your mother cordially greets you; so do Aunt Lena and your sisters and brothers, all of whom are looking forward to a successful progress and conclusion of your studies. Mother requests that you greet your teacher and his wife. Further, should they wish to be with you here during this Shrovetide, or these happy days, while I am gone from here, then this is fine with us. Aunt Lena very much asks for this.

Farewell, my son; listen to and learn for the exhortations given to you by good men. The Lord be with you.

January 27, 1537
Wittenberg

MARTIN LUTHER,
your Father according
to the flesh and spirit

The *Table Talks* represent the best of Luther's small talk. They were collected by friends of his as they met together to enjoy moments of light conversation. It is not hard to see these brief statements as passing thoughts shared around a table of good food with good friends. They are those off-the-record private thoughts not easily preserved for posterity.

These talks offer a more intimate look at Luther as he lived his life from day to day. Especially touching are his thoughts on the death of his daughter. Any parent who has lost a child will find great comfort in his comments.

It is important that we see Luther as more than an academic or reformer. He was a human being subject to the same feelings as the rest of us. His methods of expression may seem at times inappropriate, but then that was Martin Luther, a man with a heart of gold and feet of clay.

CHAPTER ELEVEN

Table Talks

LUTHER'S EVALUATION OF HIS WIFE

"I wouldn't give up my Katie[1] for France or Venice—first, because God gave her to me and gave me to her; second, because I have often observed that other women have more shortcomings than my Katie (although she too has some shortcomings, they are outweighed by many great virtues); and third, because she keeps faith in marriage, that is, fidelity and respect.

"A wife ought to think the same way about her husband."

Summer or Fall, 1531

---

[1]Luther was married to Katharine von Bora (1499–1552), a former nun, on June 13, 1525. See Clara S. Schreiber, *Katherine, Wife of Luther* (Philadelphia: Muhlenberg Press, 1954).

THE GREATEST THING IN DEATH IS FEAR

"Fear of death is death itself and nothing else. Anybody who has torn death from deep down in his heart does not have death or taste it."

Somebody inquired about the pains of death, and Martin Luther replied, "Ask my wife if she felt anything when she was really dead."[2]

She herself responded, "Nothing at all, doctor."

Thereupon, Dr. Martin Luther continued, "For this reason I say that the greatest thing in death is the fear of death. It is written in the epistle to the Hebrews [2:9], 'that by the grace of God He might taste death for every one.' We are blessed if we don't taste death, which is very bitter and sharp. How great the pain of tasting death is we can discern in Christ when He said, 'My soul is very sorrowful, even to death' [Matt. 26:38]. I regard these as the greatest words in all the Scriptures, although it is also a great and inexplicable thing that Christ cried out on the cross, 'Eli, Eli' [Matt. 27:46]. No angel comprehends how great a thing it was that He sweated blood [Luke 22:44]. This was tasting and fearing death. Creation consoles the Creator,[3] and the disciples noticed nothing of these things."

September 1542

DESCRIPTION OF THE DEATH OF MAGDALENE LUTHER

When his daughter was in the agony of death, he [Martin Luther] fell on his knees before the bed and, weeping

---

[2]The reference is to the grave illness of Luther's wife Katharine in 1540.
[3]Cf. Luke 22:43.

bitterly, prayed that God might will to save her. Thus, she gave up the ghost in the arms of her father. Her mother was in the same room, but farther from the bed on account of her grief. It was after the ninth hour on the Wednesday after the fifteenth sunday after Trinity, in the year 1542.

September 20, 1542

THE LOVE OF PARENTS FOR THEIR CHILDREN

Often he [Martin Luther] repeated the words given above: "I'd like to keep my dear daughter because I love her very much, if only our Lord God would let me. However, His will be done! Truly nothing better can happen to her, nothing better."

While she was still living he often said to her, "Dear daughter, you have another Father in heaven. You are going to go to Him."

Philip Melanchthon said, "The feelings of parents are a likeness of divinity impressed upon the human character. If the love of God for the human race is as great as the love of parents for their children, then it is truly great and ardent."[4]

September 1542

LUTHER'S DAUGHTER MAGDALENE
PLACED IN COFFIN

When his dead daughter was placed in a coffin, he [Martin Luther] said, "You dear little Lena! How well it has turned out for you!"

He looked at her and said, "Ah, dear child, to think

---

[4]Cf. Isa. 49:15.

that you must be raised up and will shine like the stars, yes, like the sun!"

The coffin would not hold her, and he said, "The little bed is too small for her."

[Before this,] when she died, he said, "I am joyful in spirit, but I am sad according to the flesh. The flesh doesn't take kindly to this. The separation [caused by death] troubles me above measure. It's strange to know that she is surely at peace and that she is well off there, very well off, and yet to grieve so much!"

September, 1542

THE COFFIN IS ESCORTED FROM THE HOME

When people came to escort the funeral, and friends spoke to him according to custom and expressed to him their sympathy, he [Martin Luther] said, "You should be pleased! I've sent a saint to heaven—yes, a living saint. Would that our death might be like this! Such a death I'd take this very hour."

The people said, "Yes, this is quite true. Yet everybody would like to hold on to what is his."

Martin Luther replied, "Flesh is flesh, and blood is blood. I'm happy that she's safely out of it. There is no sorrow except that of the flesh."

Again, turning to others, he said, "Do not be sorrowful. I have sent a saint to heaven. In fact, I have now sent two of them."[5]

Among other things, he said to those who had come to escort the funeral as they were singing the verse in the psalm, "Lord, remember not against us former iniquities" (Ps. 79:8), "O Lord, Lord, Lord, not only former iniq-

---

[5]Luther's eight-month-old daughter Elizabeth had died August 3, 1528.

uities but also present ones! We are usurers, gougers, and for fifteen years I read Mass and conducted the abominations of the Mass."

September 1542

WHAT IT TAKES TO UNDERSTAND THE SCRIPTURES

"I wonder whether Peter, Paul, Moses, and all the saints fully and thoroughly understood a single word of God so that they had nothing more to learn from it, for the understanding of God is beyond measure.[6] To be sure, the saints understood the Word of God and could also speak about it, but their practice did not keep pace with it. Here one forever remains a learner. The scholastics illustrated this with a ball which only at one point touches the table on which it rests, although the whole weight of the ball is supported by the table.

"Though I am a great doctor, I haven't yet progressed beyond the instruction of children in the Ten Commandments, the Creed, and the Lord's Prayer. I still learn and pray these every day with my Hans and my little Lena.[7] Who understands in all of its ramifications even the opening words,[8] 'Our Father who art in heaven'? For if I understood these words in faith—that the God who holds heaven and earth in His hand is my Father—I would conclude that, therefore, I am lord of heaven and earth, therefore Christ is my brother, therefore, all things are mine, Gabriel is my servant, Raphael is my

---

[6]Cf. Ps. 147:5.

[7]Luther's son John was born in 1526 and his daughter Magdalene was born in 1529.

[8]Of the Lord's Prayer. Cf. Matt. 6:9.

coachman, and all the other angels are ministering spirits[9] sent forth by my Father in heaven to serve me in all my necessities, lest I strike my foot against a stone. In order that this faith should not remain untested, my Father comes along and allows me to be thrown into prison or to be drowned in water. Then it will finally become apparent how well we understand these words. Our faith wavers. Our weakness gives rise to the question, 'Who knows if it is true?' So this one word 'your' or 'our' is the most difficult of all in the whole Scripture. It's like the word 'your' in the first commandment, 'I am the Lord your God' (Exod. 20:2).''

Fall 1531

THE STUDY OF THE BIBLE DEMANDS HUMILITY

"The Holy Scriptures require a humble reader who shows reverence and fear toward the Word of God and constantly says, 'Teach me, teach me, teach me!' The Spirit resists the proud. Though they study diligently and some preach Christ purely for a time, nevertheless, God excludes them from the church if they're proud. Wherefore, every proud person is a heretic, if not actually, then potentially. However, it's difficult for a man who has excellent gifts not to be arrogant. Those whom God adorns with great gifts He plunges into the most severe trials in order that they may learn that they're nothing. Paul got a thorn in the flesh to keep him from being haughty.[10] And if Philip were not so afflicted he would have curious notions. When on the other hand Jacob[11]

---

[9]Cf. Heb. 1:14.
[10]Cf. 2 Cor. 12:7.
[11]Jacob Schenk, an Antinomian.

and Agricola[12] are haughty and despise their teachers and learning, I fear it may be done with them. I knew the spirit of Münzer,[13] Zwingli, and Karlstadt. Pride drove the angel out of heaven and spoils many preachers. Accordingly it's humility that's needed in the study of sacred literature."

May or June, 1540

WHERE THE WORD IS THERE IS CONTEMPT

"When the Word comes, contempt for it is there too. This is certain. One can see it in the case of the Jews. God sent them the prophets Isaiah, Jeremiah, Amos, sent them Christ Himself, even divided the Holy Spirit among the apostles, who cried out together, 'Be penitent!' But nothing helped. They all had to endure much. Soon Jerusalem lay in ruin, and it remains so to this day. The same thing will happen in Germany. I think a great darkness will follow the present light, and after that the Judgment Day will come."

Winter 1542–43

MAN'S ARROGANCE AND SELF-ASSURANCE

"It's remarkable that men should be so arrogant and secure when there are so many, indeed countless, evidences around us to suggest that we ought to be humble. The hour of our death is uncertain. The grain on which we live is not in our hands. Neither the sun nor the air, on which our life depends, lies in our power, and we have no control over our sleeping and waking. I shall say nothing

---

[12]John Agricola was Luther's chief Antinomian opponent.
[13]Thomas Münzer was a radical religious leader in the Peasants' War.

of spiritual things, such as the private and public sins which press upon us. Yet our hearts are hard as steel and pay no attention to such evidence."

November, 1531

GOD'S PUNISHMENT OF THE GODLESS

"While I was in Erfurt I once said to Dr. Staupitz,[14] 'Dear doctor, our Lord God treats people too horribly. Who can serve Him as long as He strikes people down right and left, and we see He does in many cases involving our adversaries?' Then Dr. Staupitz answered, 'Dear fellow, learn to think of God differently. If He did not treat them this way, how could God restrain those blockheads? God strikes us for our own good, in order that He might free us who would otherwise be crushed.'

"When I was in Coburg[15] these comments about adversaries taught me the meaning of the words in the Decalogue, 'I the Lord your God am a jealous God.'[16] It is not so much a cruel punishment of adversaries as it is a necessary defense of ourselves. They say that Zwingli recently died thus;[17] if his error had prevailed, we would have perished, and our church with us. It was a judgment of God. That was always a proud people. The others, the papists, will probably also be dealt with by

---

[14]Luther was recalling this conversation which he had with John Staupitz (d. 1524), then vicar-general of the Augustinian Observantists in German, while Luther was still in the Augustinian monastery in Erfurt.

[15]During the Diet of Augsburg in 1530 Luther was in Castle Coburg.

[16]Exod. 20:5. In Luther's *Small Catechism* these words appear at the conclusion of the Ten Commandments.

[17]Huldreich Zwingli, the Swiss Reformer, died in battle on October 11, 1531.

our Lord God. They invoked the bread[18] as God, and now He will become as hard as iron toward them. Oecolampadius[19] called our Lord's Supper a Thyestian banquet[20] [and ridiculed participants in it as] flesh-eaters and blood-drinkers. Now we say to them "Here you have what you asked for." God has spoken once for all: He will not hold him guiltless who takes His name in vain.[21] Surely they blasphemed when they invoked God in the bread or called us flesh-eaters, blood-drinkers, God-devourers. The same will happen to our papists who have burdened themselves with the blood of the godly. God grant that by Pentecost they may be destroyed root and branch! They themselves say that they want either to smother doctrine or leave nothing behind. Amen. Let it be as they wish! How can our Lord God repay them better than by giving them what they want?"

November 1531

THE TRIALS OF A PREACHER AND REFORMER

"If I were to write about the burdens of the preacher as I have experienced them and as I know them, I would scare everybody off. For a good preacher must be committed to this, that nothing is dearer to him than Christ and the life to come, and that when this life is gone Christ will say to all, 'Come to me, son. [You have been

---

[18]I.e., the transubstantiated bread of the Roman Mass.
[19]John Oecolampadius, co-laborer of Zwingli in Switzerland, died in Basel on November 24, 1531, shortly after this conversation in Wittenberg.
[20]Thyestes was a mythological figure who was served his own son to eat.
[21]Cf. Exod. 20:7.

my dear and faithful servant]."[22] I hope that on the last day He'll speak to me too in this way, for here He speaks to me in a very unfriendly way. I bear [the hatred of] the whole world, the emperor, and the pope, but since I got into this I must stand my ground and say, 'It's right.' Afterward the devil also speaks to me about this, and he has often tormented me with this argument, 'You haven't been called,' as if I had not been made a doctor."[23]

Early in the year 1533

DO NOT DEBATE WITH SATAN WHEN ALONE

"Almost every night when I wake up, the devil is there and wants to dispute with me. I have come to this conclusion: when the argument that the Christian is without the law and above the law doesn't help, I instantly chase him away with a fart. The rogue wants to dispute about righteousness although he is himself a knave, for he kicked God out of heaven and crucified His Son. No man should be alone when he opposes Satan. The church and the ministry of the Word were instituted for this purpose, that hands may be joined together and one may help another. If the prayer of one doesn't help, the prayer of another will."

Spring 1533

WHAT IS INVOLVED IN A CALL
TO THE MINISTRY

"First of all, this is certain: young people must be brought up to learn the Scriptures. Later they will know

---

[22]Cf. Matt. 25:21.

[23]Luther often appealed to his doctor's degree as the ground for his authority to instruct and reform the church.

that they are to be educated to be pastors. Afterward they will offer their services when some position is unoccupied. That is to say, they will not force their way in but will indicate that they are prepared, in case anybody should ask for them; thus, they will know whether they should go. It is like a girl who is trained for marriage; if anybody asks her, she gets married. To force one's way in is to push somebody else out. But to offer one's service is to say, 'I'll be glad to accept if you can use me in this place.' If he is wanted, it a true call. So Isaiah said, 'Here I am. Send me' (Isa. 6:8). He went when he heard that a preacher was needed. This ought to be done.

"A young man should find out whether somebody is wanted, and then whether *he* is wanted. The latter must also be. What is to be said about talents is touched upon in the text that speaks about servants who are called.[24] It is written by Paul, 'If anyone aspires to the office of bishop, do not hinder him, for he desires a noble task' (1 Tim. 3:1). But to force one's way in is to do as Karlstadt did; during my absence he abandoned his citadel (that is, his pulpit), occupied my pulpit, and changed the Mass.[25] All this he did on his own authority. So he did also in Orlamünde,[26] and he said he wanted to give the theologians some trouble."

Spring 1533

---

[24]Cf. Luke 19:12–27.

[25]While Luther was absent in the Wartburg Castle in the fall of 1521 and the spring of 1522, Andrew Karlstadt took it upon himself to introduce changes in Wittenberg that confused the people.

[26]In 1524 Karlstadt introduced even more radical changes in the church in Orlamünde, near Wittenberg, and was expelled on account of them.

EVERY SEVENTH YEAR BRINGS A CHANGE

"My Hans is about to enter upon his seventh year,[27] which is always climacteric, that is, a time of change. People always change every seventh year. The first period of seven years is childhood, and at the second change—say, in the fourteenth year—boys begin to look out into the world; this is the time of boyhood, when the foundations are laid in the arts. At the age of twenty-one youths desire marriage, in the twenty-eighth year young men are householders and heads of families, while at the age of thirty-five men have civil and ecclesiastical positions. This continues to the age of forty-two, when we are kings. Soon after this men begin to lose their sense. So every seventh year always brings to man some new condition and way of life. This has happened to me, and it happens to everybody."

June 5, 1532

WHY GOD PLACES CHRISTIANS IN THE WORLD

"God placed His church in the midst of the world, among countless external activities and callings, not in order that Christians should become monks but so that they may live in fellowship and that our works and the exercises of our faith may become known among men. For human society, as Aristotle[28] said, is not an end in itself but a means [to an end]; and the ultimate end is to teach one another about God. Accordingly Aristotle said that society isn't made by a physician and a physician or by a farmer and a farmer. There are three kinds of life:

---

[27]Luther's oldest son, John, was born June 7, 1526.
[28]Greek philosopher (384–322 B.C.) who had great influence on medieval theology.

labor must be engaged in, warfare must be carried on, governing must be done. The state consists of these three. Consequently Plato[29] said that just as oxen aren't governed by oxen and goats by goats, so men aren't governed by men but by heroic persons."

August 31, 1538

---

[29]Greek philosopher (d. 347 B.C.) who was the teacher of Aristotle.